Journalism
Right and Wrong

Journalism
Right and Wrong

Ian Mayes

guardianbooks

For my colleagues, journalists and others,
at the Guardian

First published by Guardian Books,
an imprint of Guardian News and Media.

A CIP record for this book is available from the British Library.

ISBN: 978-0-85265-068-4

Cover Design: Two Associates
Text Design: www.carrstudio.co.uk

Printed and bound in Great Britain by William Clowes Ltd, Beccles, Suffolk

Contents

Preface

Books on journalism frequently disappoint. Memoirs can be self-serving. Academic studies are too often dominated by theory and divorced from the messy reality of the deadline and the newsroom. Textbooks can be dry, dull things.

This book by Ian Mayes is none of the above. For one thing, Ian has been a working journalist all his adult life – more than 50 years of reporting, subediting and commissioning. During this time, he has been much more interested in the nuts and bolts of daily practice than in the abstractions of media theory. It has shown in his nine years as readers' editor, placed most unusually in the no man's land between journalist and reader.

It's a pretty good vantage point. He combines an outsider's distance with an insider's perspective. He explains us to them, and them to us. Sometimes he manages the even harder job of explaining us to us. Through hundreds of columns he's helped Guardian journalists understand better how we're seen by our readers. Just as often he's done something to explain particular decisions or judgments to our readers. Occasionally he will criticise or defend an article or editorial call. More often he will simply hold it up to the light and examine it.

That weekly process of real-time mediation, examination and explanation has forged this book. There's nothing theoretical about it: every single column grew out of the dust and fracas of live journalism. This, for better or worse, is how it is.

Actually, it is both better and worse than most people – including journalists – generally believe or let on. Let's do the "worse" first. Most people in the business of news like to pretend we're humble truth seekers. We want people to believe we tell it as it is – all the news that's fit to print (or, increasingly, not print). Actually, a very great many things conspire to come between us and this admirable objective. There is seldom enough time and never enough information. More often than not there will be people trying to be obstructive, if not downright misleading. There can be logistical difficulties, faulty technology, and normal human misunderstandings. There are, in other words, many reasons why journalism falls short of its worthy ambition. Yet we still pretend that we never slip.

I don't know anyone – reader or reporter – who truly believes that journalism is anything but a blunt, imperfect tool. But very few editors behave as though it is. Clarifications and corrections on most papers are still granted grudgingly and tucked away where as few readers as possible will notice them. I think we should correct systematically and prominently. First, because it's right and fair. If we get things wrong, or not quite right, there's an ethical obligation to do something about it. Second, because owning up to mistakes makes people trust us more, not less. Third, because the zeitgeist of the digital age is increasingly about challenges to the pronouncements of old media and expectations of higher standards of accountability and transparency. And finally, because it makes a statement about the nature of the endeavour in which we're all engaged.

The "better" bit is also true. Most of my colleagues genuinely do care about getting at the truth. They have high ethical standards, they think deeply about their trade. Some of them are extraordinarily dogged, persistent and brave. Their reporting is frequently extremely robust, even when challenged most determinedly by people who want to believe otherwise. A select few of them put their lives in danger because they care about the free flow of unpolluted information. There are plenty of uplifting examples of such journalism in these pages, too.

Ian is – I don't think he'll mind me saying – a wise old bird. Most people in our trade could learn something from these little essays. Aspiring journalists could learn even more. Ian's next role on the Guardian will be to write the latest volume of the paper's history. This book is actually a fairly significant part of that recent history. And so is Ian.

Alan Rusbridger, January 2007

Acknowledgments

The first person I want to thank for her invaluable help in the compilation of this book is Charlotte Dewar, who manages to combine the roles of assistant both to me and to Simon Jenkins. The thematic arrangement of the book is hers and beyond that she has made numerous suggestions, all of which I have been more than happy to follow. It is perhaps particularly fitting with a book of this kind that I should add that any mistakes are entirely mine.

Helen Hodgson, the assistant readers' editor, has been a constant support through the thick and thin of what can be at times an extremely stressful job. I could not have shared it with anyone better and I thank her most sincerely. My thanks are also due to Murray Armstrong, my most frequent deputy, and Barbara Harper, who has also deputised for me on numerous occasions. In and out of those roles they have been sources of wise counsel and friendship.

Chris Elliott, the managing editor of the Guardian, and his principal assistant, Wendy Collinson, have been my stress-free points of liaison with the bunker — the name by which the cluster of offices around the editor, Alan Rusbridger, is known. He and they have helped no end to make it easy for me to exercise the independence that my terms of reference require. Alan Rusbridger's commitment to the idea of having a readers' editor around the Guardian has, so far as I can judge, never flagged — it was, after all, his idea in the first place. I would like to thank him for that.

Finally, my renewed thanks to the Guardian's publisher, Lisa Darnell.

1.

INTRODUCTION

This is the sixth book that has appeared under my name since I became the readers' editor, the independent resident ombudsman of the Guardian in 1997. Three of the books have been compilations of selected columns and some of the funnier corrections, the latter being a by-product rather than the main point of my activities. The other two have been collections of my weekly Open Door columns, generally dealing with ethical issues arising from the Guardian's journalism. One is published in Armenian, and aimed particularly at students of journalism in Armenia. The other is published in Russian by the Moscow Media Law and Policy Institute and is intended to introduce the concept of the news ombudsman to the many agencies in the Russian Federation now grappling with the difficulties of establishing a truly free press and looking for a system of self-regulation that might help. The Russian book, which consists solely of the weekly columns, is already in well-established use as a course book in Moscow State University's journalism faculty, one of the largest in the world with more than 2,000 students. I would like to take this opportunity in passing to thank my friend Andrei Richter, the director of the Moscow MLPI, itself part of the university, whose initiative it was to publish the book and who has ensured a wide circulation for it in the Russian Federation. In the past few years it has been a particular delight to travel in Russia sharing the experience of almost a decade in the job here at the Guardian. I have been to Rostov-on-Don and

Krasnodar in the south, to Moscow, of course, and to Nizhni Novgorod and Kazan towards the east, refreshing along the way a lifelong interest in Russian literature.

There is, in fact, huge curiosity around the world in the possibility of applying the ombudsman principle of impartially adjudicating complaints to the turbulent field of journalism. The hostility and danger of the environment in Russia was emphasised just before my most recent visit by the murder of the journalist Anna Politkovskaya, whom I remembered in my speech in Kazan. In the past decade I have travelled to most of the European countries where news ombudsmen, although increasing in number, are still sparsely scattered, but also to Argentina, Brazil and Peru, where there is real promise of development. Early in 2006 I went to India, where the Hindu, based in Chennai, became the first newspaper in the sub-continent to install an ombudsman, following the Guardian pattern. Inquiring visitors to the Guardian have come from many other countries, among them China, Japan, Korea, Romania, Bulgaria, Kenya. As I write I am looking forward to a visit to South Africa where at present only one newspaper, Die Burger in Cape Town, has an ombudsman, my colleague George Claassen. Interest in the system has grown considerably in countries with little history of freedom of speech and with a difficult political and economic inheritance. In some cases there is a long way to go before such a consensual system of self-regulation as the ombudsman (a word which covers both male and female practitioners) stands any real chance of being established.

There have been a number of reasons for the many invitations I have had to explain what this rare creature, the news ombudsman, is and what he or she does. One is the high global profile of the Guardian, read online in almost every country in the world. Another has been my role in the Organisation of News Ombudsmen (ONO), particularly in the past couple of years (2005 to 2007) when I have had the privilege to be its president. ONO, in the context I have briefly described, has enormous potential to help those who are seeking to help themselves. It requires continuing commitment and support from the news organisations — still slightly fewer than 100 around the world, the largest number in the United States — that employ ombudsmen.

The Guardian has been a marvellous place in which to practise this crude discipline and I have been very fortunate that during the entire period the paper has been presided over by the editor, Alan Rusbridger, whose idea it was to establish the role here. If the exercise of my contractual independence, underwritten by the owner of the Guardian, the Scott Trust, has ever caused misgivings he has concealed them remarkably well. He has been totally supportive throughout. You will easily deduce from some of the columns in this book that there have been moments of difference but these were never allowed to develop into real conflict. As for the Guardian journalists, I cannot speak too highly of them. I think that a good many of them — even if an email from me, or worse still, a personal visit, was received with a shiver of apprehension — came to see the system as a good thing. What I tried to do through these columns was to facilitate a conversation between the journalists and their readers that remained reasonable in tone even when the journalists' work was the subject of adverse criticism, or when, as happened quite often, the reader's complaint was in the end rejected. The demonstration that such a conversation was possible is what I think has attracted the interest of practitioners and students of journalism around the world. By opening a door into the newspaper readers have been able to discover what degree of thought has gone into specific decisions, whether the decision is seen on reflection to be right or wrong.

It is the only form of self-regulation that can, that should, have the effect of building trust between the employing news organisation and its readers, listeners or viewers. When the

Guardian has tested trust in its journalism among its own readers it has always scored extremely well: being open and accountable has, I think, played a part.

Naturally I would like this book to appeal to the reader who reads not only the Guardian but any newspaper of serious intent. I would be especially pleased if journalism students found it stimulating and I hope that arranging the subjects thematically will make it more readily useful to any of them persuaded to look into it. The fortunate ones are the inheritors of freedoms that have been hard won over long years.

The greatest source of encouragement I have had has been from the readers themselves. The book, like the journalism, is primarily for them.

2.

THE FALLIBLE JOURNAL

I have tried to keep all the pieces in this book more or less as I wrote them. What value they have derives from the fact that they were written in consideration of real issues raised by real readers. I particularly wanted to keep untouched the first of the columns you see here because it was the first one that I wrote as readers' editor and it marked the beginning of an extraordinary experience. I felt very conscious of the need to strike the right tone. It seemed to me that since I would often be considering contentious matters in a fraught, tense and adversarial atmosphere, the tone should be as close as possible to that of a calm and civilised conversation between reasonable people.

The tone, I think, has been consistent through the nine years. Much else, however, has changed in the Guardian itself, not least its size. The number of staff journalists has grown from the 245 quoted here to about 450, and the number of commissioning editors has grown proportionately. John Willis, the Guardian's external ombudsman, appointed in 1997, just before me, has not served continuously throughout the nine years. Other commitments engaged him elsewhere for several years, and he was only reappointed again in 2006 to consider, in the first place, a complaint about an adjudication of mine in a complex matter involving the American academic Noam Chomsky.

Conspicuously absent from my first column in 1997, for

obvious reasons, is any mention of the internet, which rose to become such a significant factor during the period that followed, and which we shall come to in a later section of this book. You will see that by 2003 Guardian Unlimited already had about 7 million unique users (separate individuals) a month, a figure that has almost doubled in the three years since then. In the blogging age a curious resonance is acquired by the words of John Gross quoted below, actually commenting on the rise of the printed press: 'It gave them [writers of the time] a powerful new platform, and at the same time drowned out what they were trying to say with triviality and claptrap.'

The annual number of published corrections, given below as 1,500, requires only slight amendment to 1,600 or a little over. It is in my view sufficient. It exceeds the number of truly significant mistakes the Guardian makes while falling short by an unknown number of the overall total. The number of readers getting in touch with me annually after the Guardian's change of format in September 2005 from broadsheet to the smaller Berliner almost doubled to about 18,000. In its first 10 years of existence the office of the readers' editor will have received about 100,000 complaints and queries, and substantially reduced in the process the number of people seeking to sue for defamation. The principle that this section, I hope, makes clear is that to err is human and to correct, if not divine, is always the best thing to do.

Why the readers need an editor, too

Every week the Guardian publishes a total of well over half a million words – substantially more than the number in, say, James Joyce's Ulysses, or perhaps a more appropriate example, Don Quixote. Most of these words are written against pressing deadlines. Indeed, it has been said that without a deadline the journalist finds it difficult to perform at all. As Karl Kraus, the Austrian satirist, put it: 'A journalist is stimulated by a deadline, he writes worse when he has time.' Not only the Guardian's 245 staff journalists, and not just the 70 who actually commission the material that appears in the paper, but the many freelance and specialist writers who contribute, are – most of the time – subject to the same constraints. An exception may be the investigative journalists who spend weeks, months or even longer before the results of their work appear on the printed page. But, in a broad sense, this pressure of daily edition times provides the context in which the journalist strives to be both accurate and ethical: let's say to be fair.

If anyone wanted to construct a machine for the production of errors, a newspaper would probably be it. Journalists have traditionally had what might be called a 'tomorrow is another day' attitude towards error and complaint, therefore leaving behind them what they hoped was a more or less invisible trail of unresolved, if mostly minor, grievances. The disgruntled have often been left with the options of liking it, lumping it, or turning their attention to another newspaper.

It is in an effort to counteract this, to change the culture, and to help those journalists whose willingness to deal with complaints or queries from readers has been frustrated by the other pressures upon them that the Guardian has now set up its two-tier structure for dealing with grievances.

John Willis is already in place as the Guardian's ombudsman, an independent 'outsider' briefed to handle the most serious complaints, matters, for example, where the Guardian's journalistic integrity is called into question.

And from this week, I am the readers' editor, with the responsibility 'to collect, consider, investigate, respond to, and where appropriate come to a conclusion about readers' comments, concerns, and complaints in a prompt and timely manner, from a position of independence within the paper'.

I have 'to seek to ensure the maintenance of high standards of accuracy, fairness, and balance' in the Guardian's reporting and writing.

On the subject of independence, my appointment is initially for two years, and during that time I can only be removed from the job by a vote of the Scott Trust, the proprietor of the Guardian. The content of this column, which when possible will be weekly and usually discuss aspects of readers' concerns, complaints or suggestions, is not subject to prior approval by the editor or others on the Guardian's staff.

An important part of my function, as the extract I've quoted from my terms of reference makes clear, is to gather and print corrections and this the Guardian has already begun to do under the heading 'Corrections and clarifications' (a title borrowed from the Irish Times) at the foot of the Obituaries page each day. This is the page I most recently edited, prompting one colleague to describe my new job as a move from the dead to the injured. The column has since been moved to a more prominent position on the letters page.

The corrections column itself, of course, has no immunity from error. There's a rather ominous note in Katharine Graham's autobiography, Personal History. Mrs Graham, chairman of the executive committee of the Washington Post, which in 1970 became only the second newspaper to appoint someone to a similar job, writes: 'Even corrections can be troublesome, particularly when attempting to rectify some egregious error only compounds the original problem.' It seems like a worthwhile risk to take.

In the past 30 years the idea of readers' representatives or internal ombudsmen (the name varies from one newspaper to another) has not exactly spread like a bush fire. There are fewer than 40 in the US, where there are more than 1,600 dailies. There is a mere scattering across Europe and the rest of the world.

One of the American readers' representatives observed after three-and-a-half years in her job, 'I have learned ... that it is much easier to deal with the public than it is with the newsroom, which I suspect is true because the newsroom generally is the object of challenge. Few of us take criticism truly well.' Others have described a sense of newsroom 'chill' at their approach. All those who have written about the job caution against seeking it as a route to popularity.

Why on earth do it? I believe that if it can be done well, it might go some way towards restoring confidence in newspapers and journalists, now at an appallingly low ebb, and that it would then be of benefit to us all. Here are the words of CP Scott, the great editor of the Guardian for 57 years, until 1929: 'Comment is free but facts are sacred ... The voice of opponents no less than that of friends has a right to be heard. Comment also is justly subject to a self-imposed restraint. It is well to be frank; it is even better to be fair. This is an ideal. Achievement in such matters is hardly given to man. Perhaps none of us can attain to it in the desirable measure. We can perhaps but try, ask pardon for our shortcomings, and there leave the matter.'

November 8 1997

Naming and blaming

The question of blame for errors is one I generally try to avoid, considering it the business of the daily corrections column to concentrate on, well, correcting. The idea is that the paper takes it on the chin. So expressions such as 'We inadvertently said ...', or 'We should have made it clear ...' occur quite regularly in the column, 'we' being the key word.

Following through some particularly heinous error is, it has been agreed through practice, the business of the editor and his staff. This demarcation has applied throughout the existence of the corrections and clarifications column. The aim has been to run the column in a way that encourages consensus: the consensus would be that most of the people for most of the time thought the corrections system a good thing, fairly operated.

Frustration, however, can build to the point where some unilateral action seems necessary.

One thing that I have occasionally done when an error persists, despite all efforts to eradicate it, is to correct it once more, giving the dates of all the previous occasions on which it has been corrected. This way almost all of us finally learned how to spell Lucian Freud.

I followed the same course more in exasperation at my efforts to correct the term 'industrial tribunal' in favour of 'employment tribunal', the title that has applied for about the past six years (for almost as long, in fact, as the corrections column has been running). The day that the last correction of that appeared, trailing the dates of all the previous corrections, the error occurred again with an embarrassing simultaneity on the opposite page. I sent an email to the writer and the editor asking them please to be sure not to miss that day's corrections column.

There are further turns of the screw: the correction could point at the offender by identifying him or her by title, or when all else had failed, by name. Reason, I hope, would restrain me, as it has done so far.

Pressure to go in that direction usually comes from writers and the complaint is levelled at the subeditor. Something was 'written in', introducing an error; the subeditor made a false assumption without calling the reporter for clarification; a reference was lost in the course of cutting; agency copy had been added that the bylined journalist had already considered and rejected, and so on.

What reporters really want in these circumstances is not so much for a colleague to be pilloried as to be exonerated themselves. Sometimes the reasons for doing that are strong, where, for example, an introduced error has placed the person whose name appears on the report in an acutely embarrassing or even dangerous situation, or imperils a person whose views are given in the report. This can be the case in reports filed from areas of extreme tension or conflict almost anywhere in the world. The accidental deletion of the word 'not' could do it: 'He said he was not planning sabotage.' The report is instantly available on the internet. The correction, exonerating the reporter, or getting the endangered person off the hook, follows as shortly afterwards as possible.

Corrections of this kind include such phrases as, 'in the editing …' or 'this appeared in the published version as …'

Why in my view attributions of this kind should be rare is that they can delay the appearance of the correction; they tend to be divisive (contrary to what a few insist upon, writers and subeditors are not opposing camps in battle); and corrections of this kind can still be ambiguous (was it the subeditor, or the desk editor, or even the revise subeditor who introduced the error?).

What may be unfair about corrections of this kind, if carried without very good reason, is that they say nothing about the nature of the task that confronted the subeditor. What state was the reporter's copy in when it landed on the subeditor's desk?

How many errors or infelicities did the subeditor remove before letting the story into the paper with the one mistake that remained? Did the piece need complete rewriting?

I cannot show you specific examples of pieces before and after editing because that would be unfair to the writers. But were I able to do that, your respect for the subeditor, however high at the moment, would rise.

But it is the reporter's name that appears on the story. It is the reporter who has to face the person who appears to have been misquoted or misconstrued. It is the reporter who walks out that morning feeling that his or her credibility has been dented. So sometimes circumstances will demand that the reporter should be exonerated, but not too often.

March 6 2004

Quote unquote: some memorable views on journalism

A Martin Kettle column in which he extolled the virtues of the American writer Henry David Thoreau as revealed in his Walden, reminded me recently of something Thoreau had to say in that book on the subject of newspapers: 'Why should our life be in any respect provincial? If we will read newspapers, why not skip the gossip of Boston and take the best newspaper in the world at once? – not be sucking the pap of "neutral family" papers …'

This quotation made a great impression on me more than 30 years ago partly because I had already been working for about 15 years in journalism in what were sometimes called the provinces (the company for which I worked was at one time called Provincial Newspapers). Thoreau's was one of the first of many comments on journalism, or on journalists, that I noted down as worth remembering.

It was also one of the few that could be held to say something positive about journalism, even allowing for Thoreau's implication that the 'family' newspaper, with its bland regurgitated version of things, was not worth reading at all. At least it held up the possibility of something more challenging and useful, if only we were to define it and then demand it.

Most of the comments that struck me had nothing very good to say about the business of journalism. That may be because I gleaned most of them from 'literary' sources, so in that sense they were gathered accidentally from my normal reading.

About the time that this habit was taking root Weidenfeld and Nicolson published John Gross's The Rise and Fall of the Man of Letters (1969). Gross declared: 'Journalism is a career; literature is, or ought to be, a vocation.' Gross continued, 'Few major 19th-century writers would have gone quite as far as John Ruskin, who dismissed the entire output of Fleet Street as "so many square leagues of dirtily printed falsehood", but most of them viewed the growth of the press as a very mixed blessing indeed. It gave them a powerful new platform, and at the same time drowned out what they were trying to say with triviality and claptrap.'

Journalism, the message seemed to be, was something real writers only deigned or stooped to do. The message did not seem to vary much according to time or place.

A more recent addition is from Henry James's The Portrait of a Lady, in which journalism is ironically fused or confused with literature: 'Mrs Varian's acquaintance with literature was confined to the New York Interviewer; as she very justly said, after you had read the Interviewer you had lost all faith in culture.' There is a particularly memorable line when Isabel, the heroine, accuses her friend, Henrietta Stackpole, the journalist from the Interviewer, of having no sense of privacy. '"You do me great injustice," said Miss Stackpole with dignity. "I've never written a word about myself!"'

Among the early quotations I jotted down was one from Karl Kraus, the Austrian satirist (1874-1936): 'Journalists write because they have nothing to say, and they have something to say because they write.' It came from WH Auden's commonplace book A Certain World (Faber), and spurred me on to find and read more KK, rewarding me with: 'No ideas and the ability to express them – that's a journalist.' (No Compromise, selected writings of Karl Kraus, Frederick Ungar).

Chekhov, expressing shame over some of his early newspaper pieces, wrote: 'The word "newspaper-writer" means, at very least, a scoundrel. I'm one of them; I work with them; I shake hands with them; I'm even told that I've begun to look like one … But, I shan't die as one.' (From VS Pritchett: Chekhov, A Spirit Set Free, Random House.)

I could go on (on and on, as a matter of fact). It is not all one-sided. We overlook great figures such as William Hazlitt and

Leigh Hunt. The latter, writing against slavery, said: 'The history of opinion tells us never to despair of effecting the ruin of prejudice.'

And Auden himself had particular praise for the journalist who digs out 'cases of injustice, cruelty, corruption, which the authorities would like to keep hidden, and which even the average reader would prefer not to be compelled to think about.'

This column is adapted from a talk given at the Guardian Hay festival. Martin Kettle's article about Thoreau (and Robert Tressell) appeared on August 17 2004

August 28 2004

The facts of the matter

During a recent conference with his heads of department the editor of the Guardian led a discussion about the undiminished flow of errors in the paper and the apparent resistance to our best efforts to stem it. Were journalists beginning to take the process for granted, he wondered. Was there a tendency to say, never mind the extra minute or two to check something, if it is wrong we can carry a correction? And were department heads following up often enough after the revelation of some serious error to try to find out why it happened?

The daily corrections and clarifications column now carries about 1,500 entries a year, a number that has been fairly constant for the past four years. That is because, for me and my assistant, it represents the limit of our capacity to correct and clarify. We have never corrected all the mistakes drawn to our attention, and I have been careful to point that out on a number of occasions.

This means, for the time being anyway, that it is difficult to say what effect the introduction of a new revising system on the main news floor of the paper is having. Three revise subeditors are on duty in the newsroom every day as a final check on text, headlines, captions, before a story goes to print. Between them they cover the hours from 2.30pm to 1am. They catch a great deal but clearly not everything.

Students of the corrections column will see that it would not have been possible to check many of the mistakes corrected there once the copy had left the writer. The assistant editor (production), who is the person primarily responsible for the recruitment of subeditors, says, 'We all know how to spell Alastair Campbell, but if it is a less famous person with that first name we have to assume that the writer has checked it.'

He believes the Guardian's team of subeditors – who make up about a third of the entire editorial staff – on the whole do a very good job. There are 120 staff subeditors, not counting those who work on the website. Eighty are full-time and 40 part-time. The job has never been more demanding. They are required to be expert in the new technology, to have an eye for design, to be good at English, to be able to write a succinct headline, and to be quick.

They have to work under great pressure. Those who read only the website may have only a vague idea of the enormous volume of material produced and published during a week. Today's Guardian as it appears in the UK, with all its constituent supplements, weighs around a kilogram on Saturdays. The writer who leaves the checking to the subeditors cannot know what they do.

Not long after I began this job I forecast that one of the potential threats to the effectiveness of the system as a spur to greater accuracy lay in what I called its domestication. The absence of journalists' names from the corrections column may be one of the things that encourage such a tendency. I remain totally opposed to the idea of naming journalists in the corrections column for anything other than the most heinous crimes (although I did name one recently to apologise to him for having corrected one of his reports unnecessarily).

The comedy in many of the minor corrections may be another factor: frankly I could not manage without it.

The swift post-mortem or note to offenders from the relevant desk editor should perhaps become systematic.

The most significant development, already begun and likely to continue, is the discovery of the readers' editor and the corrections column by readers of the Guardian online. The Guardian had more than 7m unique users during June (responsible for almost 83m page impressions).

Several million people are reading the Guardian outside the UK, all over the world, but principally in the US. It means, among other things, that the work of Guardian journalists is being scrutinised not only by a domestic readership for the most part sympathetic to the paper's liberal views but by people who do not share those views at all.

To put it another way, there is no foreign correspondent so remote that his or her reports will not be read immediately in the host country, and in all probability by people directly involved in the story. Increasingly, they will let the paper know what they think.

The internet has, in effect, closed the gap between home and foreign news. It has also closed the gap between the newspaper and its readers, wherever they are in the world and whether they are sympathetic or hostile. Increasingly, getting it right in the first place will be seen as the easy option.

July 12 2003

Not a house of correction

A few days ago a respected colleague came up to me in the newsroom and said with some feeling, 'That was the most thoroughgoing humiliation I have ever suffered.' He was referring to a long correction – relating to a piece he had written – which had appeared in the paper that morning.

This does not exactly make me feel good, particularly since the complainant – the person who featured in the erroneous report – conceded that the fault was not entirely ours, but partly his, a subtlety I was unable to convey in the correction. But the main point remained that the mistake was 90% our own.

The journalist involved was consulted during the drafting and redrafting of the correction. A copy of the correction was faxed to the person who complained. He faxed it to colleagues in Germany on whom our error was also thought to reflect.

I mention all this for two reasons. One, as an example of a correction that, as it went through its various amendments, needed quite a lot of time to sort out, time therefore that could not be spent on things which I necessarily deemed to be of lower priority. The other, the main reason for mentioning it, is as a partial reply to those readers who get in touch with me from time to time demanding blood. What, they want to know, happens to the people who make all these mistakes? Is anyone ever disciplined, fired, executed? Well, not really, or perhaps I should say, not as far as I know. The column is called 'Corrections and clarifications', not Crime and Punishment. The aim is to focus on the error or the source of the confusion and it is not a function of the column to pillory the individual responsible for the mistake.

The reaction I just mentioned – the feeling of humiliation, although it is subjective and not intentionally inflicted – indicates the seriousness with which one journalist regarded his inclusion in the column. It's the one spot in the paper that no journalist wants to appear in, even though it is a deliberate and carefully considered policy (mine) not to mention the names of writers in the corrections column unless, as has happened, they have a special reason for wishing to be mentioned, or if it is difficult to construct a coherent correction without mentioning them.

One particularly hideous aberration did, I know, draw a stiff letter to the perpetrator from the editor. But that, were I asked, would have to be for what was probably the worst of our sins during the past six months (I don't intend to re-run that one).

It is entirely up to the editor and those in charge of the Guardian's multifarious editorial parts whether or in what way they react to corrections. Those readers who cry for the guilty to be punished might try placing themselves in the position of the journalist who finds his or her work corrected, or criticised in some way in one of these weekly columns. To put it another way, how would you like it?

I believe that this kind of self-regulation is only possible through the large measure of consensus the term implies. The starting point has to be the assumption that we all want to be accurate and honest. Nothing has persuaded me that the case is otherwise – I am talking about intent – despite the fact that we have published more than 500 corrections and, had I been able to keep up with the demand from readers, would have published a great many more.

So far as I know the corrections column has only tripped up seriously once. That was when, in seeking to make what appeared to be a clear-cut correction quickly, I acted too hastily in taking the complainant's word for it and apologised for something that was not the Guardian's fault. This caused some grief to the journalist involved (putting it mildly) and to me too. I wrote to the complainant, the director of a prominent pressure group, making the point that if this service, which the Guardian is unique in providing, is to succeed it has to be accepted as fair by the journalists as well as by those who complain.

On at least two occasions among those 500 published corrections we have run immediate and full apologies despite, and not because of, a threat of litigation (which actually followed in one case). On those occasions we went against the opinion that many journalists still hold, that in cases of serious error it could be costly and is therefore foolish to admit guilt. We threw up our hands, accepted responsibility and apologised.

May 9 1998

3.

CREDIT &
PLAGIARISM

The basic theme of this section in one that also runs through the next section on sources, and indeed through the book: the need for the journalist to be frank and open with the reader. Deception discovered by the reader, even when it might be said to be 'harmless', is a rat that gnaws at credibility and trust. The reader, as an almost invariable rule, should be able to be confident that what he or she reads is what it appears to be, and generally that it is written by the person whose byline appears on it, and furthermore that that is the writer's real name. Some of the exceptions are discussed in this section.

It is not always possible to say in absolute terms that this way is right and that way is wrong. What I have tried to do then is to set out some of the points to be considered without coming to a conclusion. So you will see I finish the column, below, on ghostwriting, with a question: should the reader be told when this has taken place? For the sake of argument I avoided expressing my own opinion. Had I stated it, it would have been 'whenever possible', endorsing the practice of using some such form as 'So-and-so was talking to (a named journalist)', or 'as told to'.

Some US readers chastised me for being too soft on plagiarism in the column you find here, by not defining it in absolute terms and by not condemning it in absolute terms too. Defined at its worst plagiarism warrants the strongest condemnation, and no sympathy need be wasted on journalists who by stealing others' work showed themselves ready to inflict great damage on their own and their employers' credibility. Plagiarism has occurred in the Guardian during the past nine years very rarely. The point I wanted to make was that plagiarism is less likely to occur if the culture is to declare all significant sources - and that is something that the Guardian has increasingly encouraged.

If the pseudonym fits

At the ritual reading of lists at the editor's morning conference the other day, when section editors reveal a provisional schedule for their pages in the following day's paper, the comment editor almost blew the cover guarding the true identity of the Guardian's satirical columnist Norman Johnson. He checked himself after using the writer's real first name. There is no indication at the end of the regular Saturday column that Norman Johnson is a pseudonym. The picture byline is an artful part of the deception, derived from photographs of three or four different people – contrived under a special dispensation exempting it from the rule that no unacknowledged picture manipulation appears in the Guardian.

The column itself is also rightly an exception to what I believe should be the general rule: that writers should be allowed pseudonyms only for very good reasons, and that, when they are used, the fact should be noted at the foot of the article, unless it is self-evident. This is, in fact, a rule already established by practice if not by editor's edict.

Even now there remains a vague air of mystery around the name Norman Johnson (persisting even inside the Guardian), although anyone who wished to dedicate a little time to the task could soon discover the writer's real identity. Norman, if I may, follows in a Guardian tradition of anonymous satirists, among whom in recent years must be counted the well-named Bel Littlejohn.

Readers are left to become progressively aware that they are participating in a game between the paper and its readers. Very few people have seemed to mind when the light has finally dawned. It often takes some time. In Norman Johnson's case, invitations to parties, to write books, to appear on television still come in (quite recently to appear on BBC Breakfast to talk about divorce in the light of a remark in his column about 'starving harpies'). All are declined with a polite non-revelatory email.

Away from columns of this kind, it seems clear to me that pseudonyms are justified when the security of the writer is an issue, or when it is necessary to protect the employment of the writer. Almost any citizen reporting from Baghdad, for example, is entitled to whatever measure of protection a pseudonym affords. The Baghdad Blogger, who began writing for the paper under the name Salam Pax in the period leading to the fall of the city, could not have taken us into his world in any other way. Similarly the Baghdad dentist Zeyad A, a current contributor to the Guardian's Comment is free blog, has his identity protected from the complete exposure that would make our conversation with him impossible.

Erwin James, who began writing about prison life towards the end of his long life sentence for murder could not have written under his real name since that would certainly, at the very least, have complicated his relationship with his fellow prisoners.

In all these cases – cases where the pseudonym necessarily liberated the writer – the fact that the chosen name was a pseudonym was instantly apparent or stated at the foot of the column.

What should not happen is that a pseudonym is lightly conferred upon, or allowed to conceal the identity of a journalist who is writing something clearly adversely critical or pejorative about another individual. This happened recently in the Media pages, and the individual who was the subject of the piece – a columnist and blogger, who, using a pseudonym himself, expressed views that many would find abhorrent – questioned not the factual content of the report but the motive for writing it. Was there, he legitimately asked, some element of malice at work? Had he and the anonymous writer crossed swords in the past?

In the end I was satisfied that there was no malice or 'history' involved. Writer and subject have never met. I also felt that there was no convincing reason for the writer to be allowed a pseudonym. The general rule should be, if you want to say it, come out and say it.

June 6 2006

Credit where credit is due

A reader writes from Barcelona: 'I am curious to know why many of your newspaper's articles are bylined by your own editors or reporters when the news is identical to that of Reuters. I realise that [agencies] provide copy for you but I am curious as to who should claim credit for an article. Surely it should be the person who wrote it – or does the editing of a few lines of a story from [an agency] merit a byline?'

He then provided an example – a Reuters report and a more or less identical version of it bylined by a staff journalist that the reader had read on Guardian Unlimited.

'As a regular online and print reader I would just like to know where the paper stands on this?' He ended by making it perfectly clear where he stood: 'I want to know exactly who is really writing what I am reading.'

This is a reasonable, basic requirement for a reader to demand of a newspaper, isn't it? It is certainly so with regard to news coverage and should generally be demanded of features, too.

The example quoted by the reader is an undesirable phenomenon; it steps away from the direction in which the Guardian has been going in recent years and ranks, one hopes, as an aberration. The reporter has been made aware of that. His name was quickly removed from the story as soon as his editor became aware of it, and Reuters was properly credited.

Things have changed, and I think very much for the better, since I wrote about the need to give credit where credit is due in one of my early columns. I was writing on that occasion with particular reference to the Press Association, the largest agency supplying home news to newspapers in the United Kingdom and the Republic of Ireland. 'Our invisible friend,' I called it. It was then still fairly common for a PA story to appear under the byline of a Guardian reporter who had had little or no original input, and with no credit to the agency. The crude justification was that the paper bought the service to do with pretty much as it wished.

'We have been asking ourselves,' I wrote then, 'is it right?' The answer, the paper has progressively been conceding, is, 'No, it is not right.' The policy of the paper is to name not only agencies but other newspapers who have provided the Guardian with unique material: material not made generally available through a press release, a news conference or widely broadcast, for example. (There is an anomaly in that regional agencies in the UK are still rarely credited for their contributions, an omission that the paper's rights manager describes as 'a major beef' with them. He pointed out that, in the case of the larger international agencies, due credit was a contractual requirement.)

More broadly, the deputy editor told me: 'The policy is to be honest about sources and how a story has been constructed.' A Guardian byline should only be added to a report originating with an agency if the paper's journalist had made a significant additional contribution. Agencies, and newspapers too, should be identified as the source of significant contributions.

Occasionally a report will be bylined by a named Guardian journalist 'and agencies'. Not everyone likes that. One senior journalist, among the more scrupulous in identifying sources, believes this shrouds precision in fog and should be avoided where possible.

Any newspaper policy, in my experience, tends to be untidily applied. But one reason why newspapers now need to be more frank about the sources of material, should they show any reluctance, is because readers, like the one with whom I began, are demanding it: it was a reader, not the agency, who drew this particular lapse to the paper's attention, it is interesting to note. Assiduous attribution will be taken as a sign of honesty not inadequacy.

March 6 2006

The earlier column about credit and the Press Association appeared on January 30 1999

The ethics of ghostwriting

A couple of weeks ago we carried across the bottom of one of the comment pages an article by an asylum seeker recounting her experience of racism in Middlesbrough.

The council in Middlesbrough, and one of its MPs, took issue with aspects of the article, not to deny the existence of racism there but to counteract any implication of general calumny and to point to positive features. Letters from them were published and that seemed to me to have satisfied the rules of fair play.

What flowed from the article also seemed to me to be good. An important subject was aired. It was taken up by the local newspaper. Numerous offers of help were made to the named author through the organisation whose email address was given at the end of the article.

What was not given there was the name of the journalist who had interviewed the asylum seeker and written up her account – entirely with her approval and in the asylum seeker's words, I should add. In effect the article was ghosted, something that was left undeclared. Is that consistent with the paper's desire to be open with its readers? We do not acknowledge the editors or subeditors who work on an article; are ghosts different?

You could rightly hold up the case I have mentioned as an excellent example of a function the paper conceives as a duty: to give a voice to those who might otherwise not be heard. Would the account be undermined or the named author appear patronised had the editors told readers in an endnote that she 'was talking to' the journalist?

The question then arises, however, why would we do that with an article presented in this way by an asylum seeker when we do not do it in the case of politicians, for example? Part of the answer may be that with the latter we might be more aware of the common process, the likelihood that it had been drafted and gone to and fro for amendment between politician and staff before final approval and 'signature'.

The comment editor said, 'If we were to ask, say, the same journalist to interview another asylum seeker and she were then to use all the asylum seeker's words and the asylum seeker were to agree the text, in what sense is that not the asylum seeker's piece? The only difference I can see with the trade union official, museum director or politician [who employs an adviser or press officer] is that the journalist is not employed by the asylum seeker, but by us. At what point does editing fade into ghosting?'

The paper has no stated policy on ghosting and is inconsistent in the way it declares or does not declare when it has taken place. It is a device used from time to time in most departments of the paper, certainly in features, the arts, and sport.

If you browse in the sports section of a big bookshop you will find plenty of 'autobiographies' of sports celebrities which declare the name of the collaborator, often prominently – on the cover, for instance – with the tag 'as told to', or 'with' so-and-so. Ghosted columns in the sports pages of newspapers, on the other hand, rarely carry any declaration, and that is true of several in the Guardian.

The sports editor said: 'The reason we do not include an endline is that the words come from the bylined personality and are approved by him/her or representatives. In this way they are not different from [comment] columns written by advisers on behalf of politicians or administrators.' He said it was a good way of getting interesting material from sportspeople, who would not have time to write them. 'The ghost transcribes their thoughts, the columns are then passed to, say, the athlete or his or her agent, for approval before going into the paper.'

The features editor estimates that he runs a ghosted piece about once a fortnight. 'The key principle that should apply, I think, is that our ghosts are essentially doing a job of transcribing and editing, not writing. When we ask writer X to ghost a piece by Y, we expect the language to be Y's not X's. Shuffling the order of what they say, tidying sentences, finding a good way to begin and end are all fine – we do that in editing any written piece.'

To my mind ghosting in the form of extended first-person transcriptions by a journalist should fulfil at least three criteria: it should be done with the knowledge and consent of the subject; it should be in the subject's own words; it should be seen and approved by the subject before publication.

Which brings us back to the question: should the reader be told?

July 24 2004

Two accusations of plagiarism

Plagiarism is an ugly, tainting word, not to be used hastily or lightly. I have considered two accusations of plagiarism this week. One proved to be totally unjustified. The other came down to the reprehensible, if common, failure to acknowledge the source of several passages in a piece.

These were readily identifiable with the article from which they came, as much by the language in which they were written as by their content. They contained what are sometimes described as 'signature' phrases from the original.

That complaint has been the subject of a note in the corrections and clarifications column this week which named the writers of both articles and included an apology to the author of the original piece and the magazine in which it appeared. The marked departure from best practice which these unattributed borrowings represent is dealt with in the Guardian editorial code under the heading 'Plagiarism'. It says: 'Staff must not reproduce other people's material without attribution. The source of published material obtained from another organisation should be acknowledged including quotes from other newspaper articles …' This section, like others in the code, although it does not specifically say so, is meant to apply not only to staff journalists but to freelance contributors (the writer of the article under discussion was a freelance).

Even so, some caution should be exercised in applying the term plagiarism. Plagiarism, so strong and damning a term, should, in my view, be restricted to the wholesale appropriation of another's work, or to something close to it – or to put it more bluntly, to theft where the intention is clearly to deceive.

There is a greater readiness to use the term in the United States, where plagiarism, in the media and in academic life, is said to have reached epidemic proportions. The editor of the

New York-based magazine that was the source of the appropriated passages believes I should apply it in this case. I abstain from doing so not from any want of rigour. I believe the matter should be considered in its context and measured against a scale of seriousness.

I do not consider it to be first-degree plagiarism. In considering a scale of plagiarism, the capital offence would be where the plagiarising writer has done little more than replace the name of the original author with his or her own. At the lower end of the scale is the deeply embedded practice of simply lifting without attribution from 'cuttings', or now from the much more readily available electronic equivalent. Journalists sometimes call this process 'research'. It often involves the relaying of unchecked facts from sources not shared with the reader. The practice has hung around historically like an occupational disease. A great deal of energy has been spent at the Guardian in trying to eradicate it. It is probably ineradicable.

To come back to the particular case. The Guardian piece was wider in scope than the article from which the passages were taken. The responsibility for the appropriated passages appears to lie not entirely with the author of the Guardian article. One reference may have been written in by the commissioning editor in search of a legally safe expression to satisfy the Guardian's lawyers. This may be neither here nor there to the complainant. Whether or not plagiarism is the appropriate word, the complaint was essentially upheld.

The other complaint, as I began by saying, was entirely rejected. I have pointed out before that all complaints coming to me by email – unless the sender requests total privacy, or the content clearly demands it – are received in a queue which is available to all staff journalists at their desks. This one carried in the header the advice: 'Complaint and documentation about plagiarism by [a senior Guardian journalist] on the story about a 12-year-old Muslim boy held at gunpoint.' The sender then listed close similarities in content between a report dated August 26 in Muslim News and the Guardian report, dated, he said, August 28.

There was however one flaw. The Guardian piece appeared not on August 28 but on July 28, a month before publication of the article the Guardian journalist was accused of plagiarising. I pointed this out to the reader. Then in the ensuing silence I wrote again, wondering whether he might apologise. He did.

September 3 2005

4.

SOURCES

The columns in this section are concerned mainly with sources but also with other broadly related matters such as declarations of interest. Again it all comes down to what the newspaper tells the reader, what kind of relationship the newspaper wants with the reader. The need to declare an interest might be expressed in the form of a reader's question to the editor: 'Is there anything you should tell us about the writer of this article that might be relevant to our assessment of its contents or the views expressed in it?' As one of the columns dealing with such declarations shows, it is not always a simple matter and can lead to claims that the declaration was prejudicial, intrusive or even racist.

Although these columns make clear the desirability to declare sources whenever possible, they also look at issues such as the journalist's responsibility to protect the identity of confidential or anonymous sources when it has been necessary to use them. One of the questions explored is: Is such protection an absolute duty? The Hutton inquiry mentioned a couple of times in this general context was concerned with events surrounding the death of Dr David Kelly, a Ministry of Defence employee and expert on Iraqi arms, who died following the revelation or leaked revelation of his identity as one such confidential source.

The columns also touch on the vulnerability of the newspaper when anonymous sources are relied upon, when anonymity can be used by the source to test public reaction to a proposal which can then be officially denied if the reaction proves to be adverse.

Not least of the matters discussed, I suggest, is the degree of responsibility incurred by the reporter, and by the newspaper, to vulnerable subjects chosen to illustrate some general misfortune or problem. The case here is how and with what justification the Guardian used the story of Grace Matnanga to highlight and make personal the problem of Aids in Malawi, and by extrapolation throughout sub-Saharan Africa. I can tell you that the journalist concerned did keep in touch with Grace, that Grace's own treatment for HIV has continued, and that she herself now works for an Aids clinic, helping others.

Declarations of interest

I have been dealing with a complaint from someone who had been interviewed by a freelance writer compiling a piece about wind power for our Weekend magazine. The complainant – who belongs to an organisation, Country Guardian, which opposes the development of wind power, on environmental among other grounds – felt that in the finished article, which appeared last weekend, his views were inadequately represented.

He asked whether we knew that the author of the piece had a professional interest in promoting wind power as the editor of the quarterly magazine of the European Wind Energy Association, something the complainant himself had only discovered after being interviewed. The answer was no, we did not.

It is clear, reading the article, that the author is an enthusiastic proponent of the development of wind power who believes that any environmental disadvantages are greatly outweighed by the advantages. He concluded his piece by saying, 'Country Guardian has already signalled its opposition to offshore wind farms and is ready to campaign against the first firm proposal. Yet Britain is the windiest country in Europe. If we cannot exploit our most abundant natural fuel source, what price our commitment to the environment?' The author has written about wind power for the Guardian before. He felt his interest and point of view were already known. He says the idea of mentioning his freelance job as editor of the magazine of the European Wind Energy Authority did occur at the time he was seeking the commission but he decided it was not a significant point. He felt that his own view would be apparent in the piece and that that in itself would constitute a frank enough declaration of interest. This is a view not shared by at least one of those interviewed who feels that he should have told him of his interest at the time he sought an interview.

The piece that the writer presented initially, according to the editor who commissioned it, was entirely in favour of wind power and other views had not been consulted. Since the editor knew the issue was controversial, she asked the writer to do it again, seeking and including contrary views. This resulted in the piece more or less as it was published, still without any declaration of the writer's interest.

There is nothing wrong with publishing pieces written by partisan writers (a paper that didn't would be dull indeed). The piece in question, as I have said, was clearly partisan. In it, we were at least told that strongly opposing views existed. However, the fact that the writer neglected to tell us – and that we therefore were unable to tell our readers – of his interest had the effect of calling into question the credibility of the piece and the paper among those who knew of this connection. One of these was the first person who complained.

By agreement, the complainant expressed both his frustration and the view which he had hoped to find put over in the Guardian Weekend article, on the letters page of the main paper. He accepted this as a satisfactory resolution of (what I considered to be) an important dispute.

We try to ensure that the relevant interests of someone writing for the Guardian are declared at the end of the contribution. This is done habitually on the comment pages, in the Society and Education sections, and elsewhere as thought appropriate. The question for a freelance is whether an undeclared interest, if discovered, is likely to be used to embarrass the writer and the Guardian by sowing seeds of doubt about a perfectly sound and legitimate piece.

It should be the task of the commissioning editor to resolve any doubt about whether an interest should be declared or not. The test is whether, in the form in which an article is presented, the reader will know where the writer is coming from, if that is relevant to the content.

This was a test we were accused of failing (by two rival newspapers, but also by a number of individual readers) in the presentation of our reports exposing as a fake the Carlton TV programme The Connection. We began publishing these reports on May 6 and three days later, on May 9, we carried on page 2 an 'Editor's comment', clearly stating the background of the two freelance journalists mainly responsible for the reports. We also declared that the articles had not been timed to influence competition between Granada and Carlton for a new current affairs programme.

We probably should have carried something like this from the outset, if only to introduce writers likely to be unknown to the vast majority of readers. I do not believe it touched the integrity of the pieces. The sceptical reaction that the absence of a declaration sometimes prompts is one that, in ourselves, we always consider healthy.

May 23 1998

According to a source

The Guardian, like all other newspapers, carries stories from time to time that depend on a single unidentified source. What are the journalist's obligations to the source? All journalists recognise a duty to protect the identity of a confidential informant; it is their side of the bargain. But are there any circumstances in which the name of the source might be disclosed, and if so to whom?

Few if any would feel the contract between journalist and source was void if the information provided turned out to be wrong, which it sometimes does. The paper then faces the embarrassment of a retraction and apology, and a dent in its credibility.

But what if it becomes clear that the source lied? 'In that case,' one Guardian journalist said, 'all bets are off.' Even so, no one I asked this week could cite an occasion when a lying source had been exposed. Perhaps journalists are restrained in those circumstances by the knowledge that their own judgment has failed. One journalist said his obligation to protect the identity of the source was the same whether the source lied or not. Either way, the responsibility was the paper's.

I am prompted to raise the subject by a recently published letter from Tim Crook, a senior lecturer in media law and ethics at Goldsmiths College, University of London, commenting on aspects of the Hutton inquiry. He wrote: 'Protecting a source is without qualification. It should never be given up – not to the editor or proprietor; not even after death. Journalists should never identify confidential sources on any traceable record, without the knowledge and permission of their informant.'

The deputy editor (news) asks several questions of a reporter when assessing a contentious story that depends on an anonymous source. Is the source personally known to you? Have you had previous dealings with the source, and has the information passed on been accurate? Is the person in a position to know or assert what he or she is telling the paper?

He said: 'If the answer is yes to all of those questions we may be satisfied but there are occasions when, because of the seriousness of the story and the impact it will make, the journalist volunteers the name of the source to emphasise the weight of the story. Never has the name leaked out subsequently.'

The executive financial editor said there were some highly sensitive sources he had carried from paper to paper. 'I would not reveal them to anyone, under any circumstances – whatever the consequences.' That would be his position, he said, whether or not he risked going to jail, or blighting his career.

However, he added: 'A blanket statement that sources remain confidential to the one journalist working on a story at all times, in all circumstances, just doesn't fit with the complex reality of producing news.

'Stories, certainly big important stories, are rarely produced by one reporter working in isolation. There is a constant discussion between editor and reporter on how a story is pursued, written, projected, and that can lead to the editor learning which sources are being used – without even [asking for] the information.'

He said he would never demand the identity of a source from a reporter. 'But, when necessary, I would expect assurances from the reporter on the type and quality of source being used and, on some occasions, on a confidential basis, this may lead to me being given the precise identity of the source. The reporter would automatically expect the information to go no further in any circumstances, and I would naturally honour that.'

The security of the source's identity in this case depends on the trust that exists within the paper between reporters and editors, a point made by the editor of the Guardian. He said he did not think he had a right to know the identity of a source although he was happy to receive the information when it was offered to help in the process of evaluating a story – and in exceptional circumstances he might ask for it. If a reporter refused to give the name, then the editor was left with all the other factors in making his assessment, one of which would be the track record of the journalist. 'I don't think I have a right to know but I am entitled as editor not to run a story or to run it less prominently or to soften it.'

What is at stake is the credibility of the paper. How reliable is the source? More importantly, can you believe what you read?

September 13 2003

Responsibility after the event

I recently wrote about Saving Grace, the Guardian's 12-page broadsheet supplement on Aids, which posed the question: why can't Grace Matnanga, one of the million people with HIV in Malawi alone, get the drugs she will need to stay alive? I explained how the supplement was planned, and how and why Grace Matnanga was chosen to represent and to make personal the plight of all the others.

Grace does not look ill at the moment. She confronted readers in a close-up photograph covering the entire upper half of the front page of the supplement. The photograph was taken in the market place of her village with about 50 people crowding round, curious to know why Grace was suddenly the focus of such attention.

Was that Grace's moment? Did the Guardian incur any special obligation to Grace in using her in this way? If it did, has it already discharged it by telling her story? And what are the feelings of journalists in these situations? Where does the story end for them?

The effectiveness of the presentation in this case, avoiding emotive 'victim' pictures, reflecting the even tenor of the health editor's text, has been borne out by the reaction to it. An adviser to the government of Malawi said: 'At last, at last someone has presented the situation on the ground in a manner that does the issues justice ... You have done Malawi, the people of developing countries, and the cause of international health an enormous service.'

The part that Grace played was obviously very significant. The head of UNAIDS in Malawi praised the 'unique' way chosen 'to present and humanise the statistics and sufferings of the people'.

The supplement, it is clear, not only performed the primary function of informing the debate. It also moved a large number of you to want to act, in many cases specifically to help Grace. In an article on Friday, headed, 'What you can do to save Grace', the health editor referred to her own dilemma and her instinct to help, not immediately Grace, who does not yet need medicine, but another woman in a much more advanced and serious condition.

She explained why directing funds at specific individuals was difficult and could cause bureaucratic problems for already overburdened Aids workers. It would be better, she accepted, to make a donation to an organisation that is at work in the field, perhaps the Lighthouse Aids clinic attached to Lilongwe central hospital in Malawi, the clinic that will be trying to help Grace when the time comes.

The editor of the Guardian believed that the paper had honoured its responsibility to Grace, which he recognised, through its reporting of her story. Furthermore, it had a continuing commitment to stay with the Aids story. 'I think we could be criticised for not telling readers when the supplement was published how they could help. But you have to accept that our job is to raise these issues and report them.'

He said he completely understood how reporters working on stories such as this developed a personal involvement and commitment to the people they met. 'I think if individual journalists are moved to do something they should do it. You would be an odd human being if you didn't.'

Several Guardian journalists whom I consulted thought the paper had incurred a special responsibility for Grace. 'It's an exception [but] there's something about the prominence with which we used Grace, her image and, most of all, her name, not only to project the powerful and important message that the [articles] carried, but to project the Guardian, which [would make] it, to my mind, wrong to walk away for ever and leave it there.'

The environment editor said he did not believe the paper itself had any duty to make a donation. It was a matter for individuals.

However, he had on one occasion 'donated' Guardian money. 'I saw a particularly obscene well in Bangladesh that was a source of diarrhoea and other diseases. It transpired it would cost just £60 to clean it up. I gave the money to a local NGO and they got to work immediately. When I got back I put it on expenses as "£60. Drinks for 3,000 people."' He thought contact should be maintained with Grace and specific help offered when it was needed.

March 3 2003

From the horse's mouth

There is nothing like a good quote to enliven a story, to take the reader closer to the action, to give a report that first-hand sense of immediacy and authority that is – unless I am getting carried away – the essence of journalism. But beware the reporter who inquires, 'How lively would you like it to be?' Anything that appears between quotation marks and is attributed to a real person should be the actual words spoken. You can take that as a rule. Journalists are not expected to respond to the pressures of competition with rival newspapers, the pressures from commissioning editors, or even to their own natural desires to scintillate, by inventing quotes.

The manufacture of quotes, time-saving, story-enhancing though it may be, usually reflects a tendency to treat real-life people as though they were fictional characters invented by the journalist to do with as he or she pleases.

That way lies the hall of mirrors, and that is not the way we are supposed to be going. We are supposed to be stepping firmly in the opposite direction, where things are indeed what they appear to be and where we are as open and frank as we can be about the sources of our information.

A couple of recent things prompted these thoughts. The first was the Oscars ceremony earlier this week. Everyone wanted quotes, no matter how banal, from the stars. In pursuit of this our own reporter was told by a public relations consultant to come back if he got stuck and a quote would be provided: not, it was tacitly understood, a quote that had ever passed the lips of the star in question but certainly one that she might have said, and that the PR was authorised to utter on her behalf. It was not an offer that was taken up, and in the absence of direct access to the star a quote was taken from a radio interview (we did not reveal that in our report, as we should have).

This kind of collusion, between the star, let's say the 'personality', the PR or press officer, and the journalist is not uncommon in show business. That may partly explain why actors confronted in television interviews with some statement attributed to them ask, 'Did I really say that?' Well, perhaps not. That's show business. Does it matter? Our arts reporter says he himself is aware of slightly different rules in the coverage of the entertainment end of his job and the serious stuff of arts politics at the other end but tries to apply the same standards across the spectrum.

The other thing that cropped up was this: we got into a bind because one of our reporters working on a story attributed a statement to, let us call him the principal, when the words had come not from him but from his press secretary.

The principal, on this occasion, complained that he had not spoken to the reporter in question and that he had not authorised anyone to say, on his behalf, the words attributed to him. His press secretary insisted that she had not said them either. The words appeared in the paper, clearly stated between quotation marks. The reporter said he had been under the clear impression that he had been left free to extract from his conversation with the press secretary a quote to be attributed to the principal. He said it was not altogether unusual for people under pressure from the press to authorise an intermediary to speak for them, and in certain circumstances to license the journalist to use the quotes as though they had come straight from the horse's mouth.

The quotes would then be used, attributed directly to the principal, without any accompanying note – without what someone described to me as clutter – such as: in a statement, so and so said ...

On this occasion everyone thought they were right. I thought we were wrong and we printed an apology. The big test is whether what we do serves the trust that the newspaper seeks to foster between itself and its readers. This time it didn't. I have to say, though, that in five months of listening to complaints this is the only one of its kind so far.

Endless discussion is possible on variations of the rule I mentioned at the beginning of this piece. To what extent may quotes be 'tidied up' grammatically, or tightened to make them more direct and to the point? Couldn't this be done within the same rules that you would apply if translating from a foreign language? Should the omission of words or phrases within a quote be indicated, for instance by three dots ...? Since an important part of the journalist's job should be to give a voice to the inarticulate, how far should this be done by summarising someone's views in the form of a quote? There is a long-discredited but still used journalistic device where the quote the journalist wants is put to the person being interviewed in the form of a question. All that is needed is a yes or no for the whole thing then to be used as a direct quote.

Much discredit has accrued through sloppy quoting.

March 28 1998

Between the quotation marks

A few days ago someone who had figured in a report in the Guardian got in touch with me to complain that she had never uttered the words that had been attributed to her. She objected strongly because the comment, presented as a direct quotation – that is between quotation marks – was a strong one, appearing to indicate an attitude on her part which she was simply in no position to adopt (whether she wished to or not). In the controversial situation with which the story dealt it was potentially very embarrassing.

I asked the journalist concerned to ring the person he had quoted, to discuss the complaint and then to come back to me. It is not unknown – ask any reporter – for a person who is surprised by the reaction to something he has said, to protest that he never said it at all.

I did not expect that to be the case here, and it was not. The journalist conceded that the words were his, used in a question put to the person who complained. When I wrote before about the need for the reader to believe in the authenticity (and perhaps the veracity) of remarks enclosed in quotation marks, I made the following comment: 'There is a long-discredited but still-used journalistic device where the quote the journalist wants is put to the person being interviewed in the form of a question. All that is needed is a yes or no for the whole thing then to be used as a direct quote.'

It works like this: the journalist asks the person being inter-viewed, 'Do you have aspirations to run the company?' The person replies, 'Well, I wouldn't say that.' He then finds himself quoted as saying, 'I have no aspirations to run the company,' something which might conceivably prejudice his chances of promotion.

More frequently it happens in crisis situations where the question might become, 'Were you horrified by what happened?'

and the answer, 'Well, yes,' leads to the direct quotation, 'I was horrified by what happened.' Occasionally the quotation might be attributed to someone to whom the journalist has not spoken directly at all. 'Is he horrified by what has happened?' 'Yes, he is.' It then appears as, 'Mr So-and-so said, "I am horrified by what has happened."'

The practice of printing interviews in the form of questions and answers is a useful discipline that has practically disappeared from British journalism, although many European newspapers preserve it. In any case, it is generally used in more leisurely areas and not in the heat and haste of news where the kind of thing we are talking about usually seems to occur.

It is an honourable task of the journalist to render the inarticulate articulate but this is not the way to do it. It may be defended in the journalist's mind by the rarity with which anyone actually complains. In some areas the person to whom the quote is attributed, through the offices of a press officer, perhaps in effect colludes in a deceit upon the reader.

The journalist takes a chance that the words he attributes to the person who has not uttered them will be close enough to what might have been said to avoid complaint. We are only one step away from the entirely fictitious quote. One journalist told me that on the newspaper where she trained useful quotes were always attributed to a fictitious person living in an actual street in the area, one so long that in the absence of a house number no one would ever find out.

All this belongs to a culture that we should have stepped firmly away from. It runs counter to the openness and accountability that the Guardian wants to characterise the relationship with its readers. The editor, emphasising the issue of trust, wrote recently, in a slightly different context, 'If a reader reads something in direct quotation marks in the Guardian he or she is entitled to believe that the reporter can vouch for the accuracy of the quote.'

The point he was making was that if the quotation is not delivered directly to the journalist whose name appears on the report then we should state clearly where it came from; for example, from this or another newspaper, or from the radio or television.

Whether it is the case or not, the absence of such attribution makes it look as though the journalist is intending to give the impression that the quotes are freshly made. If there is inordinate use of appropriated quotes another issue is also raised, that of plagiarism. The choices and decisions are simplified by thinking of the reader.

November 25 2002

Arguments for anonymity

On Tuesday this week the Guardian ran, across the top of its front page, a report headed: 'Israel trains US assassination squads in Iraq'. One reader quibbled with the headline: the story, he said, made it clear the training was taking place in the US rather than Iraq, even if that was where the squads might eventually operate.

The sense of the headline was clear enough, I think, and right on the main thrust of the story, which was that US assassination squads designed to operate in and from Iraq were being trained by Israel.

Another reader had, on the face of it, a more serious complaint about the same piece. 'When Guardian journalists crib entire articles from other sources, perhaps they should quote their source – in this case the New Yorker magazine – slightly higher in the story than the 18th paragraph?' That comment, to put it mildly, was more than a bit unfair.

The reader quoted the website of the New Yorker, which had posted on December 8 an article by Seymour Hersh entitled 'Moving targets – will the counter-insurgency plan in Iraq repeat the mistakes of Vietnam?'

It did indeed cover some of the ground trodden in the earlier report. The New York Times has also been reporting aspects of the story from early November. The Guardian correspondent told me: 'I did some calling around on Monday and had much of the story before seeing Hersh's piece, which made my heart sink because I knew some people would assume what the reader thought.'

The point about the Guardian's report was that it was based on the correspondent's own sources and moved the story on. I have read the New Yorker report and I have discussed the handling of the story with the editor on the foreign news desk who liaised with the reporter. The mention of the New Yorker in the piece seems to me to be placed fairly and appropriately.

What interested me much more about the Guardian report was the description of its two anonymous sources. One was described as 'a former senior US intelligence official', the other as 'a well-informed intelligence source in Washington'.

On the day the report was published the editor of the Guardian held a pre-arranged meeting with the paper's news staff to emphasise his guidelines on, among other things, anonymous quotes. He had called it in anticipation of the publication of the report in January of the Hutton inquiry into events surrounding the death of Dr David Kelly.

His briefing notes, circulated earlier, struck a chord: 'Hutton may well have uncomfortable things to say about the way we gather news: how we evaluate and edit it and how we react when challenged as to its veracity. The public, already pretty sceptical about what we say and how we operate, will, I think, expect some evidence that journalists are putting their own house in order.'

The report stands up well to the test of the editor's guidelines. To quote him again: 'We have a policy on sources. It says we should use anonymous sources sparingly. It says that we should – except in exceptional circumstances – avoid anonymous pejorative quotes. It says that we should avoid misrepresenting the nature and number of sources, and that we should do our best to give readers some clue as to the authority with which they speak.'

After the meeting, one journalist said, yes, we have good rules, but maybe we should spell out to readers that they have been applied. 'For example [in the front-page report], we might have stated that intelligence sources cannot normally be identified but that the two sources used were independent of each other and had proved reliable in the past. It would be helpful to readers and would enhance credibility.'

The story of the alleged assassination squads depended on anonymous sources and without them it could not have been published with the form and force it had. Similarly, a front-page story on December 5, flagged as a 'special investigation' and concerning arms sales by BAE Systems, also depended upon anonymous sources.

To return to the editor's briefing: 'People will frequently only say interesting and important things if they can do so anonymously. Sometimes the reasons are ignoble (cowardice). Sometimes they are noble (whistleblowing).' Much, he added, had to be left to the judgment of the reporter.

It comes down to trust again and whether it can survive the healthy scepticism of the reader. Most of the time it can. Occasionally we fall flat on our faces.

December 13 2003

Disputes over description and disclosure

On December 19 2003, the Guardian carried a report by one of its political correspondents based on a speech in the House of Commons the previous day by the Labour MP for Liverpool, Riverside, Louise Ellman. The opening paragraphs read: 'A Labour MP yesterday sparked a furious row by using parliamentary privilege to claim that the Muslim Association of Britain, which helped to organise this year's anti-war marches, supports terrorism.

'In a Commons speech, which is protected from libel proceedings, Louise Ellman accused the association's senior spokesman [the Palestinian-born academic Azzam Tamimi] of inciting racial hatred against British Jews after he allegedly voiced strong support for Palestinian suicide bombers.'

Dr Tamimi, whose response was sought by the Guardian correspondent, accused Mrs Ellman of 'abusing parliament' and he challenged her to repeat her remarks away from the shelter of parliamentary privilege. The day the report appeared, the correspondent received an email from the Muslim Council of Britain, which includes among its affiliates the Muslim Association of Britain, to which Dr Tamimi belongs.

The email suggested that Mrs Ellman's background was relevant to the report and should have been mentioned. The Guardian correspondent forwarded this to me, with the remark: 'Unfortunately the subeditors removed my description of Mrs Ellman as a member of the Labour Friends of Israel group and a campaigner against anti-semitism.' I agreed that his description of Mrs Ellman was fair and relevant and should have been left in. The Guardian's policy is that details should be given when a failure to do so could cause embarrassment on subsequent revelation.

On January 3, I put the following note in the corrections and clarifications column: 'The published version of a report, headed "Muslim backs terror, claims MP" did not make it clear that the Labour MP Louise Ellman, whose Commons speech was quoted, is a member of the Labour Friends of Israel group and a campaigner against anti-semitism. It should have done.'

Mrs Ellman made no objection about this to the Guardian but it was queried by several others, including the chair of Labour Friends of Israel, James Purnell MP. Mr Purnell wanted the policy clarified and some reassurance that in this case it had been fairly applied. There was a suggestion, not from Mr Purnell or Mrs Ellman, that the note in the corrections column, for which I was responsible, had the purpose of identifying Mrs Ellman as Jewish and that the motivation for it was anti-semitic. Mrs Ellman, when I spoke to her this week, said she would have had no problem at all had the deleted details remained in the report, as they were true.

On at least two previous occasions (October 19 2000 and January 17 2003) the corrections column has been used to point out Arab sympathies. The more recent of these read: 'We should have mentioned that ... the author of the article headed "False witnesses", page 24 (Comment), yesterday, is an executive member of the Council for the Advancement of Arab British Understanding.'

There was a lull in the correspondence until the publication on February 13 2004, of an article by Sir Menzies Campbell headed, 'We must act now over Israel's wall'. Sir Menzies was described as 'the Liberal Democrat deputy leader and foreign affairs spokesman'.

Several of the correspondents who had questioned the reasons for the note about Mrs Ellman now wrote to ask why we did not tell readers that Sir Menzies received funds for the provision of research services from the Liberal Democrat Middle East Council, which in turn gets some funds from the Council of Arab

Ambassadors in London. (The Middle East councils are comparable to the Friends of Israel groups and were set up to ensure that the Arab position was fairly represented.)

Sir Menzies declares these connections in the register of MPs' interests. We told readers who raised this point that Sir Menzies was writing as a frontbench spokesman for the Liberal Democrat party and that we would not list the affiliations of any member of the government or official spokesperson if they were expressing party policy in a contribution to the comment pages.

You may or may not think the distinction is a fair one.

March 13 2004

Truths off the record

When someone tells you something it is not unreasonable to inquire, 'Where did you hear that?' We try to be helpful. I am told (by a source close to the editor) that we once attributed information in a story to 'a senior source close to an official figure' – thus, presumably, removing any doubt, for a day at least, that our reporter was right there in the thick of things.

Sometimes we can use a code and collude in the conceit that we do not have the key to it. So, 'the Downing Street spokesman' is, everyone knows, Alastair Campbell, Tony Blair's press secretary; 'a Downing Street spokesman' is one of Mr Campbell's assistants. Although the issue has been blurred this week with the publication of two admonitory faxes to ministers from, so to speak, Mr Campbell in person, there is an advantage in adhering to the code. We know the 'spokesperson' is speaking for the prime minister. When Mr Campbell is Mr Campbell is he speaking for Mr Blair or Mr Campbell?

We aspire to a condition where everything is clearly sourced. But if we relied only on information that could be attributed to a particular person, even to an unnamed spokesperson, there would often be serious restrictions on what we were able to tell you.

The unattributable remark is a way of conveying useful information that, our political editor suggests, we all take advantage of from time to time. His example, 'Your mum's in a terrible mood, but don't tell her I said so.' The same journalist recalled a conversation with Chris Patten in Hong Kong which went something like this: 'Do you want an on-the-record interview?' The journalist's reply was, 'I know what you'll say on the record; I'd prefer to know what you really think.' The beauty of the unattributable statement from the point of view of the person making it is that it can be denied if the need to do so arises. Unattributable or off-the-record statements are often used by the people making them as a way of getting deniable information into circulation so that the reaction to it can be tested. Flying kites. A famous example comes from Henry Kissinger's shuttle diplomacy in the Middle East when the thoughts of 'a senior official on Dr Kissinger's plane' were often given currency. Kissinger himself, of course, had been speaking.

What is source for the goose is not necessarily source for the gander. Here is a political sourcing problem that prompted a complaint a couple of weeks ago. Tony Blair was asked in the Commons whether Robin Cook, then on his way to Belgrade, would tell Slobodan Milosevic that Britain would 'not stand idly by' (the questioner's words). Mr Blair replied that that was the message Mr Cook would give. We then wrote in a leader that Mr Cook had delivered 'what was called a tough message that Britain "will not stand idly by" – whatever that may mean'.

The next day there was a call from the Foreign Office with a (mild) complaint that they had no recollection of Mr Cook using the phrase anywhere. He had not. Were we right or wrong? The answer is: wrong. The words directly quoted were not Mr Cook's, nor even those of Mr Blair, although he had agreed in advance that they expressed the sense of what would be said by Mr Cook. We could simply have said that Mr Cook had delivered a tough message that Britain would not stand idly by. No quotes, no complaint (although maybe still no readily discernible meaning).

When unattributable information is being given it is important that the journalist is as satisfied as it is possible to be with its authenticity and has – again if possible – an idea of the motive behind its release, whether or not this is then revealed to the reader. Our security and intelligence specialist says, 'All sources have motives. Journalists should as far as possible understand those motives to help them form a judgment about the source.' One of our leading investigative reporters says, 'The journalist must make a judgment about the informant and the quality of the information, because anonymous remarks can be used to spread false or malicious information about an opponent. The practice (of using sources) is open to abuse. Unscrupulous journalists can claim to have sources when they do not. They may put words into the mouth of sources which make sense within the context of the piece but are fictitious. The areas here are often uncheckable – royal stories, stuff about spooks, police.'

One senior editor said, 'We don't always ask who the source was. You trust the reporter. You ask, "How well do you know the source? Have you worked with this source before? Is this source in a position to know what he or she is telling you?"' We could and should be franker about most of our sources. That would still leave the need for some who serve our need to know to do so anonymously.

April 4 1998

5.

LITERARY MATTERS & REVIEWING

How does the Guardian review its own? Or even, *should* the Guardian review its own? I have not attempted the calculation, but Guardian writers probably produce more books in the course of a year than those on any other mainstream paper in Britain. The first piece here is about a highly critical review of a work of fiction written under a pseudonym by one of the Guardian's senior commentators, a review which did not get on to the page. In my view, and I am pretty sure in the view of those who decided not to run it, it should have appeared. In the event it did get reviewed more favourably elsewhere and was recommended by the hosts of a television book club. The second piece concerns an extract from a novel by David Lodge and the subeditor's decision to change Lodge's carefully chosen way of referring to Henry James as 'Henry' throughout, to the very thing he had chosen to avoid, the formal 'James'. David Lodge, while condemning the error, commends the correcting column in his The Year of Henry James: The Story of a Novel (Harvill Secker, 2006).

A review too close to home

A couple of months ago the literary section commissioned the crime writer Michael Dibdin to review a book called The Righteous Men, by Sam Bourne. Sam Bourne is a pseudonym for one of the Guardian's senior columnists, Jonathan Freedland.

The review when it arrived was what is commonly called a stinker; so much so, in fact, that the reviewer thought it necessary to attach a note which read, in part: 'It's pretty harsh, I'm afraid. If this is a problem for you or anyone else at the paper I'll settle for a modest kill fee, but it really is the most awful tosh.'

The literary editor was sufficiently exercised by this health warning to take the fairly unusual step of discussing it with the editor of the Guardian. She pointed out to him the option that the reviewer had thoughtfully suggested, of accepting a kill fee. A kill fee is a sum, usually less than the full fee agreed for a published article, payable in certain circumstances to the writer of a commissioned piece that is written but rejected.

The editor of the paper discussed the issue with several senior members of his staff, including Jonathan Freedland. He decided, after these discussions, that the literary editor should pay the reviewer the kill fee. What Michael Dibdin received, in fact, was the full fee that he would have been paid had publication of the review in the Guardian gone ahead.

A version of this sequence of events appeared in the satirical magazine Private Eye. Dibdin, a regular reviewer in the Guardian, reacted quickly to this with an email to the literary editor: 'Dear C, The latest issue of Private Eye has just arrived here … and I was shocked to discover a para about my Sam Bourne review on the "Street of Shame" page. Please be assured that I was not the source for this, any more than I was for the Times Diary piece.' He added: 'I completely understand why you decided against publishing, and indeed had said in my original submission letter ... that I would be happy to accept a kill fee if it proved awkward for you. I've enjoyed reviewing for the Guardian and have no wish to become persona non grata there, particularly over such a trivial matter as this.'

Private Eye had reported that an editorial edict had forbidden Dibdin to darken the doorstep again. In another email to the literary editor, Dibdin asked, 'Is it true?' She wrote to him reassuringly, 'I'd definitely like you to do Niccolo Ammaniti and have put you down for it.' She emailed the editor and Jonathan Freedland making clear her intention to continue to commission reviews from Dibdin.

The Times Diary item, mentioned by Dibdin, above, had indicated the customary pleasure that one paper enjoys in the difficulties of another. More to the point, it had coincided with the publication in the Times of the review that Dibdin had offered to the paper after its rejection by the Guardian. Whether or not Dibdin broke some tacit understanding implied in a kill fee that the piece should not be offered elsewhere, seems to me to be not point. I do not think the payment of a kill fee implies any such embargo, unless some special provision has been agreed.

The editor of the Guardian says that had Dibdin not volunteered to withdraw the review and accept a kill fee, the paper would have published it. Jonathan Freedland also believes that Dibdin's offer was the key factor. He added, 'It would probably have been wise to ignore his offer and publish it ...' That now appears to be the view of everyone involved, and it is certainly mine.

Michael Dibdin does not see it as a crisis. 'I want to say there is no animus in this. I admire Freedland as a journalist and I like his columns. I'd also like to say that I did not offer the rejected review to the Times in anger. I was not angry then and I am not angry now. I spent a lot of time on the review and I just wanted to see it published.' Freedland says, 'Anyway, the book is out there now and has received at least a couple of good reviews to balance his.'

April 10 2006

The importance of being Henry

Last Saturday the lead feature in the Review section was an extract from David Lodge's new novel, Author, Author, in which, as the heading said, he 'weaves fact and fiction' to explore the private life of Henry James, and in particular his friendship with George du Maurier. It commanded the cover of Review with a portrait illustration, and three whole pages inside. The keywords here are 'extract', 'novel' and 'fiction'.

There was an immediate response from David Lodge: 'You have given me a magnificent spread in today's Guardian, beautifully illustrated.' However, his email continued: 'But why oh why did you change "Henry" to "James" throughout, and without consulting me? It makes the discourse sound like biography, which was just the effect I was trying to avoid.'

The intimacy and familiarity conveyed by the use of the first name rather than the surname was something carefully judged by the author to be appropriate to the fictional focusing of the work through 'the consciousness and point of view' of Henry James. It is used almost throughout the novel.

The change was made, in fact, by a subeditor on Review without reference either to the editor of Review or to the author of the piece. The change was not detected by the section editor when the proofs were read. Both have apologised to David Lodge. The following note appeared in the daily corrections column on August 17: 'In an extract from David Lodge's novel Author, Author, about Henry James, we changed the writer's use of the first name, Henry, to the more distant and detached second name, James, thus altering the tone of the fictional piece and making it appear more like reportage. Apologies.' A correct version has been put on the website.

The first thing to be said is that there is no rule in the stylebook that sanctions such a change. Even if the stylebook expressed a strong preference for surnames in some situations – in news reports, for instance – one would need to question its application here. Indeed, the authors of the stylebook in their introduction make a point of saying, 'the unthinking application of any style guide will create more errors than it avoids – these recommendations must always be applied with common sense, and (almost) all the rules may have to be broken at some time or other.'

One of the stylebook's authors added, 'Nowhere does it say in the guide to use surnames like that (though we discuss honorifics) and certainly not in a work of fiction. It's so obvious what not to do that we didn't think it necessary to point it out, but maybe in the next edition we should include an entry on extracts, saying leave well alone.'

More importantly, Review has a commendable rule, the application of which has played an important part in establishing the good relationship it enjoys with its contributors. That is that significant changes are referred to the editor of the section and back to the author. That clearly should have been done here.

Whether communication failed at some point in the handling of this particular piece I do not know. It is certainly a question to be asked. Another question might be: are we making too much of it? Since the extract preceded publication of the book by some weeks it was a mistake unlikely to be noticed or even to be sensed by more than a very few readers, if any. The fact remains, however, that it intruded upon and distorted the relationship the author wanted to establish with his subject and with the reader. The change perhaps seems a particularly strange one to make in a work of fiction, but it would, I think, have been just as ill-advised had it been an extract from a biography of Henry James in which the author had chosen to refer to him throughout as 'Henry'. It is the author's privilege.

The editor of Review says, 'David Lodge is an internationally respected writer and a valued contributor whose relationship with Review has been built on the fact that we have treated his work with care and respect. No copy from any contributor is regarded as "untouchable" but any changes, in fiction or non-fiction pieces, should be made in consultation with our contributors.'

An 'edited extract', by agreement, may be cut to size, and have the addition of any necessary explanatory notes to make clear what would otherwise be apparent only to a reader of the whole book. Taken further, the extract may cease to be an extract and become something else.

August 21 2004

6.

PAYMENTS TO CRIMINALS

The columns here are presented in the order in which they appeared. The first, in which I argued that there were certain circumstances in which it is right to pay a criminal, or someone with a criminal conviction, for writing for the paper, was written before the Guardian began to run a regular column, 'A life inside', by Erwin James, who was then in the final years of a life sentence for murder, which he has now completed. The experience of reading Erwin James and of knowing him, as I think you will see from the open letter to him that formed the column reprinted in this section, impressed me deeply and confirmed me in the view that there were circumstances in which paying a criminal to write was the right thing to do.

The question now is not whether a criminal should be paid for his writing but where you draw the line. In the view of the Press Complaints Commission the Guardian stepped over it when it paid a criminal to write about life in prison with Jeffrey Archer. Was the criminal in this case profiting from his crime? It is a matter of interpretation and not a straightforward one. I abstained from a view at the time and I am still not sure what the right answer is in this particular case. Sometimes there is not one.

When crime can pay

Does the Guardian pay criminals to write for it? Yes, it does. Should the Guardian pay criminals to write for it? That is a matter for debate, but I think the answer to that is probably yes, too, in certain circumstances.

Recently we published an article by a convicted drugs smuggler, Howard Marks, which he had been asked to write in return for a payment of £300. In his article, Marks discussed the decision by the newly appointed Conservative health spokesman, Alan Duncan, to withdraw from the paperback edition of his book, Saturn's Children, a chapter in which he had argued for legalising the distribution and consumption of drugs.

Marks's background was thought to qualify him particularly well to comment on this. The editor responsible said: 'I wanted someone who was pro-legalisation to review the chapter and tell us what he thought.' Marks's qualifications include a sentence in the United States of 25 years in prison for smuggling marijuana, later reduced to 20 years, of which he served a third before his release in 1995. Last year he applied (unsuccessfully) for a job as Tony Blair's drugs 'tsar'.

Since his release from prison, he has written on a number of occasions for the Guardian, for payment, and in 1996 we carried extracts from his autobiography, paying fees to his publisher.

Immediately after publication of his most recent piece, I received an email asking, 'Does Howard Marks write articles for the Guardian for nothing (Saturday section, June 13, page 3)? If not, and he is paid, how is this compatible with the PCC Code, section 16(ii)?' This is the code of the Press Complaints Commission, with which all newspapers in Britain voluntarily agree to comply. Abiding by the word and the spirit of the code is intended as an earnest of our commitment to self-regulation.

The part of the code cited deals with payment for articles, and says, 'Payment or offers of payment for stories, pictures or information must not be made directly or through agents to convicted or confessed criminals or to their associates – who may include family, friends and colleagues – except where the material concerned ought to be published in the public interest and payment is necessary for this to be done.' The public interest is then defined to include: detecting or exposing crime or a serious misdemeanour; protecting public health and safety; preventing the public from being misled by some statement or action of an individual or an organisation.

This is not considered by the editor and other journalists at the Guardian to whom I spoke this week to be the most helpful part of the code. It is inadequate as a guide for editors dealing – as in this example involving Howard Marks – with a criminal who has served his sentence and, eschewing any return to criminal activity, appears to be developing a career in journalism. (Would a journalist who acquires a criminal conviction be expected thereafter to pursue a different career?) The editor of the Guardian believes the intention of this part of the code is to stop – and rightly so – a criminal deriving direct benefit from the crime (difficult enough to interpret). However, he thinks a convicted criminal should be able to use the experience he has acquired to further a public debate on an issue of importance, of which the use and abuse of drugs would be one, and that where the contribution to the debate is made in an article for a newspaper, then payment should be made.

According to the code, a criminal conviction is a criminal conviction, no matter when or where it was acquired. It makes no reference to periods of time after which the restrictions it imposes may lapse. It makes no reference to geographical factors: does a criminal conviction in another country have the same force as a conviction acquired in Britain?

Our crime correspondent believes there is often a rehabilitative factor which should be considered. He puts it in the form of a question: Would you rather have the criminal writing for the paper, or shinning up the drainpipe and removing your valuables? The code on this issue does need attention. At the moment newspapers, in deciding each case on its merits, are left with too little guidance. They should – and here I agree completely with our crime correspondent – consider the nature of the crime and convictions and the effect of the crime on its victims, and they have to judge how far any conclusion reached would be acceptable to their readers. They may still do the wrong thing.

July 4 1998

Open letter to a fellow Guardian columnist

Dear Erwin, I enjoyed meeting you and talking to you in prison the other day. Forgive me for using your pen name rather than your real name but since I have chosen to write to you in the slightly awkward form of an open letter, I thought it better to address you by the name you have used to sign the fortnightly column – 'A life inside' – which has been appearing in the Guardian (in the tabloid second section, G2), for more than a year now.

In that time you have won many fans both outside prison and inside. I was amused to hear that some of your fellow prisoners have adopted the nicknames you have given them in your column. And I know one of the letters you have had was from a lawyer who said he had been waiting for 50 years for someone to write about prisons in the way that you do.

I can understand that reaction. Over the years I have read a great deal about prison, both fact and fiction, but nothing quite so straightforward and direct and often very moving as the scenes from prison life that you give us, and certainly nothing like it in a newspaper.

Apart from the fact that you write enviably well you do it with an easy and unaffected humanity. I don't think we have to know much about prison life to see this as something quite remarkable, reflecting credit on you but also on many of those who have been responsible for you in various prisons. It speaks volumes about the long, long journey that you have made and, I know you would agree, which you could not have made if you had not confronted your crimes and the effect of what you did on others; if you had not, so to speak, faced yourself as you were.

As you know, when we carried the first of your regular 'dispatches on prison life', in February last year, we prefaced it with the note 'Erwin James has to date served 16 years of a life sentence for two murders.' And we have always added a line pointing out that you do not get paid for your contributions. The form this takes now is a note at the end saying, 'Erwin James is serving a life sentence. The fee for this article will be paid to charity.' In fact the money goes to the Prisoners' Advice Service, which you nominated and which has helped you in the past.

When readers have questioned me about these arrangements I have written privately to them, saying, among other things, that they seem to me to have been made in an exemplary fashion, with the full cooperation of the Home Office and with a lot of care and thought by the features editor of the Guardian and his colleagues.

One or two readers have seemed inclined to believe that the arrangement for, let's call it, non-payment is one imposed by the Guardian to exploit your situation to the paper's advantage – journalists are not exactly near the summit of public esteem. In fact, earlier this week I spoke to the writer who introduced you to the Guardian, and he said that he had advised you not to accept payment and you had agreed – before either of you knew that the rules, in any case, forbade it.

So far as we are concerned there are two sets of rules to be considered. The first are the prison rules which contain a straightforward ban on the transmission by convicted prisoners of material intended for publication in return for payment. The others are the self-imposed rules set out in the Press Complaints Commission code, which all newspapers say they will abide by. The relevant bit of this bars payment to convicted criminals 'except where the material ought to be published in the public interest and payment is necessary for this to be done'.

I don't believe that this applies, or was ever intended to apply, to the kind of thing you have been writing for the Guardian, or for anything similar that you might write after your eventual release. Suppose, for example, that you wrote a column called 'A life outside' about the trials, if that's not too evocative a word, of adjustment. In my mind there is no reason why an ex-prisoner should not be paid for that kind of thing. You do not write about your crimes. You certainly do not glamorise crime in general.

It sounds patronising to talk about the rehabilitative value for you of your writing. You told me how good for you it has been writing the column. But perhaps we should talk about the value of what you are doing for the rest of us.

I know that a former governor of a prison where you spent some years has said you are the only prisoner he has kept in touch with in his retirement. Your probation officer, just about to retire, told me that he will give you his home address and an invitation to keep in touch with him when you meet for the last time in prison.

I look forward to reading you in future, so don't stop writing.

Best wishes, Ian Mayes

May 19 2001

The price of the inside story

For those of you who have missed it, there has been a lively controversy – not entirely over – following an adjudication against the Guardian by the Press Complaints Commission for paying a criminal to give his account of life in prison with the Conservative peer Jeffrey Archer. The adjudication was seen as unfair and anomalous not only by the editor of the Guardian but by the editors of four other broadsheet newspapers.

The criminal in question, John Williams, a lifer released on licence earlier this year, is making a career as a writer. He is the author of two books, both of which have been serialised on BBC radio. He was paid a standard freelance fee for a diary, which, it was argued in part-justification, was somewhat in conflict with an account already published in another paper by Lord Archer himself.

The article and the adjudication are easily found on the Guardian website if you search for John Williams. I urge readers to read both and then to turn to the code (www.pcc.org.uk) that the PCC decided had been violated.

Clause 17 of this code, covering payment to criminals, is in the opinion of many, including me, in urgent need of clarification. Its primary purpose, it has been assumed, has been to prevent criminals from benefiting from their crimes by selling their stories to newspapers. It has a public interest qualification, one clause of which would allow payment if publication countered some misleading statement or action by an individual or organisation.

There are, very clearly, circumstances in which it is perfectly proper for a criminal to be paid for contributions to a newspaper. One of these is when the criminal, while serving his sentence, has developed skills as a writer, which open to him the possibility of a career in authorship or journalism.

In the light of the PCC adjudication the Guardian sought

clarification with regard to the regular column, 'A life inside', contributed to the paper by Erwin James, who is now in the pre-release phase of a sentence for two murders, after 19 years in prison.

Martin Narey, when he was director general of the prison service, wrote in a letter to James: 'Like many readers of the Guardian I have been fascinated by your diary ... You do a remarkable job of capturing the immense difficulties of long-term imprisonment and the terrible uncertainty facing lifers.'

A book of Erwin James's columns is now recommended reading in at least one prison both for young adult life prisoners at the beginning of their sentences and for staff.

A leader in the Guardian, commenting on the adjudication against it, said that if the interpretation of the PCC code threatened the publication of Erwin James's columns the paper would take the unprecedented step of withdrawing from the PCC. 'It goes without saying that no newspaper could remain part of a body which sought to prevent James, or other such prisoners, from writing about prison life, nor to deny them the honest rewards which they are entitled to expect (in James's case, with the full agreement of the prison authorities).'

The PCC has hastened to declare that it sees no conflict between clause 17 of the code and Erwin James's columns. It has expressed surprise that the Guardian should think that it might.

Anxiety over James's columns is a reflection of the value placed upon them. They draw a stream of appreciative comment. I get letters from readers seeking to be reassured that the Guardian is not exploiting the writer. The paper, in fact, could not pay James under prison rules (Standing Order 5) until October 2002. Since then he has been paid a standard freelance fee. In addition he will receive the royalties from his book.

Until last October Erwin James's fees were paid on his nomination to the charity Prisoners' Advice Service, which already this year has dealt with more than 8,000 telephone calls from prisoners (the prison population stands at 74,000).

Erwin James said: 'The PCC has in effect decided that I am doing a legitimate job, earning honest money – not "cashing in" or profiting from my crimes. Instead of learning to be a plumber or a bricklayer or an accountant, I am just a writer trying to build a career.'

August 2 2003

7.

COVERING CONFLICT & DISASTER

This is a substantial section because it includes several – by no means all – of the columns I have written discussing complaints about the Guardian's coverage of the Middle East, in particular of the Israel/Palestine conflict. Discussion of the latter is nearly always problematic because in parallel with the real conflict in which lives are lost on all sides there is a propaganda battle in which rival lobby groups (a term to which some of them object) seek to persuade the media to their points of view. It is a disproportionate struggle in which the dominant force is mounted by the pro-Israel lobby. Accusations of anti-Semitism are commonly thrown, and I have discussed these on several occasions. The Guardian is clearly interested in the plight of the Palestinians: a common accusation is that this blinds it to the difficulties faced by Israel. The columns reproduced here are concerned with the discussion of specific complaints and will, I hope, indicate the seriousness with which they are considered from whatever direction they come. However, the question I invite readers to consider about electronic lobbies, not just in the context of the Middle East, is whether they are an effective way of representing complaints, or whether they undermine themselves by seeking to subvert free speech, and whether therefore in the long run they are more likely to be counterproductive than persuasive.

I hope it may be useful to read these columns in the context of others dealing with the Guardian's coverage of calamities elsewhere in the world. The ferry disaster off the coast of west Africa, for instance, in which some 750 people died, is among a number of events calling into question the relevance of news values applied in the age of global communication. It raises the question of how we define foreign news. There is another factor that should never be far from out minds when evaluating and criticising news coverage, at least in newspapers, and that is what I call the customary turmoil in which news is gathered and processed against deadlines. To that may be attributed the painful juxtaposition of a back-to-school advertisement with coverage of the horrific school siege in Beslan.

Many of the articles in this section address a question at the heart of journalism: what to include and what not to include. The comment pages are fertile ground for this debate, and two columns look at criticisms leveled in their direction. One discusses the decision to run a long extract from one of Osama bin Laden's tapes as an article in the pages. In the column, I make use of a device I have used on a number of occasions, an internal poll of Guardian journalists, asking, what do you think? Was it right or wrong to do that?

Senegal: a distant disaster

A little over a week ago, on September 28 2002, we carried at the foot of page 15 of the main paper a report headed: 750 feared dead as ferry sinks. The report itself amounted to 320 words. Two days later, again on page 15, we carried the only other reference to it in the printed paper, a news brief (47 words) with the heading: Ferry death toll nears 1,000.

This prompted a reader to ask, 'How does the Guardian decide the relative value of news stories? [These] people, presumably black and relatively poor, died in a horrific ferry disaster off the coast of west Africa ... How would the substitution of "white", "wealthy", "cruise ship disaster" and "coast of Florida/Italy" ... affect the level and nature of coverage in the paper (as well as other media)?'

Perhaps more appeared in other sections? Well, no. The Weekly carried a brief of 32 words. The website considered but did not pursue an idea to set up a piece on the safety of ferries. In the end it did not add to the accounts that had appeared in the paper.

The first of these was written by a Guardian correspondent whose name but not location appeared on the report. In fact he was in Harare, the capital of Zimbabwe, more than 3,000 miles away on the other side of the continent. His account – as it acknowledged – was compiled from agency reports.

I do not usually compare the Guardian with other papers but here it might be helpful. The Times, Telegraph and Independent all dealt with the disaster in a similar way – on their foreign news pages. On the first day, a Saturday, the Times led page 24 with the story and a picture of grieving relatives; the Telegraph ran it across the top of its second world news page, page 19. The Independent carried a brief report on page 18. The Sundays (the Sunday Telegraph, the Observer, the Independent on Sunday and the Sunday Times) all treated it in the same way – as a brief.

We might have been applying the satirical set of relative news values put forward by Michael Frayn – a former Guardian and Observer journalist – in The Tin Men (Collins, 1965). 'A rail crash was always entertaining ... Even a rail crash on the continent made the grade provided there were at least five dead. If it was in the United States the minimum number of dead rose to 20; in South America 100; in Africa 200; in China 500.'

The striking point about the ferry disaster was, as I have indicated, the similarity of coverage, leading to the conclusion that it was assessed from a common set of news values.

The implication in the reader's question is that whatever the factors that determined the coverage and presentation, racial attitudes played a defining role. Certainly one does not have to think long about the kind of coverage the disaster would have got if any of the reader's suggested substitutions were made. A senior editor pointed to the recent extensive media coverage given to an engine fire on a ferry in the North sea where there was no loss of life. The Zeebrugge ferry disaster of March 6 1987, when the Herald of Free Enterprise capsized with the loss of 194 lives, was mentioned. Roughly five times that number died off the coast of west Africa. The question the reader is asking is: do their lives have a different value? The answer may be no but the signal sent out sometimes says yes.

It is not easy. The editors involved in news judgments of this kind say they are the most difficult decisions they have to take, never absolute and very often controversial. Columns could be filled with apparent anomalies (closer to home, consider the attention given to a train crash against that given to road accidents which cumulatively kill a much greater number of people).

One assessment that editors must make is the degree to which readers of the newspaper will identify with the victims and relatives. Will the reports have relevance for them? Will interest diminish with distance (not considered an impediment in the case of the Australian bush fires)? Is access a problem? Senegal is a former French colony. Did that affect our level of interest? Does the newspaper have a duty to raise awareness – as in cases where relief efforts follow?

I read the agency wires. Little was added that was not in the Guardian's two reports. No reporter was dispatched. We did not tell readers why the number of people on the boat was almost twice that for which it was built, or why the passengers were travelling from southern Senegal to the northern part, or what compensation their families could expect. We did not discuss safety issues. We kept our distance.

Are we working with a set of realistic news values, or have they failed to change in a changing world?

October 7 2002

Beslan: window on a hideous world

Complaints about the Guardian's coverage of the horrific events in Beslan have been relatively few. One might assume from this that the enormity of the event checked the critical hand, or even that there was a tacit sympathy with the paper's struggle to relate and comprehend such an event. No more than 20 complaints reached me. Perhaps this was also partly because the coverage, although extensive, was as decently restrained as it could be.

In at least one respect the coverage was too restrained for a few readers. Several took strong objection to the use of the term 'militants' rather than 'terrorists' to describe the hostage-takers, the immediate perpetrators of the atrocity. These complaints were provoked in particular by a heading across the top of two pictures from the hostage-takers' video: 'Inside terror school – film taken by militants shows hostages' desperate plight'. A briefly immoderate email from Nevada in the United States, for example, ended: 'These guys are terrorists, not militants, not fighters. They are terrorists!'

The term was not entirely absent. An article on the comment pages on September 6 (Max Hastings: 'These terrible tactics may actually be working') was unequivocal and right in applying it to the hostage-takers. One can still say 'right', I think, in the knowledge placed before us in more than one of the contextual and historical pieces carried by the Guardian, that a huge number of children have been among civilians killed by Russian forces in Chechnya.

Most of the complaints were from readers of the printed paper, which – almost unbelievably – carried at the bottom of a page devoted to the disastrous ending of the siege a 'back to school' advertisement. It was a deeply regrettable collision between the normality of school routine and the horror of what had happened in Beslan on which all editorial minds at work on that page were concentrated. We can agree with the reader who said: 'Please, please take more care over this kind of thing.'

There was an isolated complaint about a cartoon carried on the main comment page (Martin Rowson, September 6). Beneath the line 'How to achieve freedom and justice ...' it showed – against the background of an inferno – the figure of death placing its hand on the shoulder of a crouching gunman to whom it is saying: 'No No No! Aim lower or you'll miss the kids.' The reader found this extremely offensive and suggested that had it been British children slaughtered we should not have been so callous as to publish anything like it. I can understand that view but I cannot agree with it. The cartoon seemed to me to be an expression of proper outrage and helplessness.

A headline in an early edition on September 7 – 'Mother left daughter at captors' mercy' – drew complaint from another reader who argued, in this case quite rightly in my view, that it implied 'a voluntary abandonment' while the story made it clear that it was nothing of the sort. It was changed for later editions.

Most of the complaints were directed at pictures, in particular one used across six columns on the front page of September 6 showing the mother of 12-year-old Erik Varziyev weeping over his body during one of the many funeral ceremonies. One reader wrote: 'This seems to me to go well beyond the bounds of ordinary decency.' And another: 'We do not need to see pictures to understand how cruel and tragic the situation in Russia is.' One reader complained that the privilege of choice over whether to expose her own children to such images had in effect been removed from her by carrying the picture on the front page. 'Maybe you think that the children in this country need to share every last detail of an event so unbelievable that most adults are having a hard time comprehending it.'

Readers expect us to have carefully considered the images we show. We recently asked 2,500 Guardian readers to respond to the following statement: 'I am concerned that children should not be exposed to certain violent images.' Forty-nine percent agreed it represented their view; 28% disagreed; and the rest neither agreed nor disagreed.

The picture editor said, 'I have spent the past three days looking at horrific pictures [among several thousand images received from Beslan in that time] and this was not one of them. The question we have to ask ourselves is how to do we face up professionally and privately to increasingly horrific events in the world?' Is the newspaper a window or a screen?

September 11 2004

The Wests: unsavoury extracts?

Last Saturday, and on Monday and Tuesday of this week, we ran extracts from Gordon Burn's book Happy Like Murderers, about the killers Fred and Rose West. We bought the right to serialise the book from the publisher, Faber and Faber, with the express purpose of boosting our circulation as we emerged from the dip of the holiday season to face the rigours of competition through the autumn and winter.

There is nothing wrong in principle with that. The only thing that could be wrong would be the selection of a book in the value of which we had no real conviction. It would be wrong if we chose a book, hypocritically or cynically, for its promotional potential, knowing that the content was incompatible with the paper's real position. Some readers think that's what we did. We didn't.

Between 20 and 30 of you wrote and rang, to protest. Possibly half of that number, having seen our advance publicity, or heard our radio advertisements, complained before publication had actually begun. The latter were repelled by the very idea of revisiting the scene of the crimes in Cromwell Street and several, taking a cue from our published trails, cancelled the paper on the days the extracts appeared.

Some other readers managed the first extract in the Guardian Weekend magazine and then cancelled the paper to avoid the following two. Here's the view of one reader who did that: 'Your publication of [these] extracts ... sickens me. What hypocritical rubbish to try to justify it ... It is just another example of the Guardian's increasing obsession with violence and sensational sex.' One writer accused us of pursuing our desire to gain readers, regardless of the 'suffering, despair and pain involved in the subject matter'. Another reader felt that the extracts, which she had read, simply encouraged a prurient interest and failed to provide the enlightenment promised in our blurbs. This was her real complaint. She felt she had been led to wallow purposelessly in the mire.

The most serious attack on the series came not from outside the paper but from within. The editor of the Society section, at the paper's main morning conference on Tuesday, when the final extract had appeared, said he had learned absolutely nothing that he had not already known from the coverage of the trial.

He strongly believed that the Guardian should only publish this sort of material for one of two reasons: to show how severely disturbed people could get into a position where they were able to inflict so much damage, or to point to faults in our social structures which might be corrected. His criticisms, like all the others, were not aimed at the book (which he had not read) but at the selection and content of our extracts.

What had our blurbs been saying? Saturday's said, in part, 'Happy Like Murderers is an angry, unflinching book which documents not only the stark moral blankness of the Wests themselves but also the wider social malaise in Britain which sheltered and protected them for so long.' On Monday we said more or less the same. I could equate that with what I actually read.

This was paraphrasing the views in what I thought was a strongly persuasive introduction to the extracts, written by the former editor of Guardian Weekend (now the literary editor of the Guardian) and carried in the magazine with the first extract.

'Can it be that we deal with the discovery of such horror by employing the same strategies by which these horrors went unsuspected for so long? Can we turn away?' She concluded, 'This book asks us to accept that these things can happen. Because by knowing they can happen we make it less likely that they will.' Her conviction in the usefulness of the exercise is not shaken by the negative response to the extracts. The overall response was positive. It did boost circulation. Last Saturday sales were up by around 30,000, a significant part of which the circulation department attributes to the extracts and attendant publicity. This does not make what we did right. But the author of our introduction again: 'If we had been interested only in boosting circulation this is not the book we would have chosen.' It was a difficult and discomfiting book for that purpose.

Richard Northen, a history student from Leeds University, who spent two days in my office at the beginning of the week, felt we were right to publish and that we did so in a dispassionate and unsensational way, avoiding the risk of offending those merely flicking through the pages of their daily newspaper. 'The images on the relevant pages were disturbing only in the context of the article,' he thought.

Would I have voted against publication? With a certain unease, no.

September 12 1998

Sins of omission

Complaints about things that do not get into the paper are often difficult to deal with. Almost everything that happens every day fails to make it to the printed page or the website. What you get – in the Guardian's judgment – is a selection of the most significant details of the most significant events. It is always open to question and sometimes, on reflection, the paper admits it got it wrong.

The paper is challenged not simply for the omission of an event but on its motives for not covering it. The complaint itself is often motivated – as I have discovered – by an unshakable conviction that the omission is a deliberate act in an unstated agenda, either of the particular journalist or the organisation as a whole.

Why was the march against the war in Afghanistan in October last year not covered? The editor frankly said: 'Not to have covered that march was our mistake.' I wrote about it at the time. One or two readers were not convinced – or rather they remained convinced that the paper had deliberately neglected to cover the march since it ran contrary to its support for military action.

Why, I was asked last week by a reader in Israel, had the paper not reported a rally of about 2,000 Arabs in support of Saddam Hussein in Gaza City on September 10? A piece of unidentified copy, quoting Associated Press, followed the question: 'Did this story appear in today's Guardian?'

The answer is no. The Guardian's correspondent that day was, in any case, busy on the West Bank. The question was really intended as a statement – that the coverage was so slanted against the Israelis and in favour of the Palestinians that a report such as this, judged by the reader to reflect unfavourably on the Palestinians, stood no chance of appearing.

In fact, an electronic search failed to find any mention of it in any national newspaper in the United Kingdom.

Occasionally, a journalist, having read the day's corrections, will tell me I am making a rod for my own back. Perhaps I am.

A few days ago I finally agreed, at the request of this same Israeli reader, to run a note in the corrections column – I hesitate to call it a 'correction' – on a point in the valedictory dispatch by our former correspondent in Israel. She had written, 'after September 11 ... Palestinians and Israelis held candlelight memorials with astoundingly similar placards: "We know how you feel, we are victims of terrorism too."' The note in the corrections column, written after consultation with the paper's correspondent, repeated that passage and added: 'We should have mentioned what we reported at the time, that there were some Palestinian demonstrations of a limited nature showing apparent jubilation at the events.'

I carried this note because I perfectly well remembered the report that had appeared in the Guardian at the time and I felt sure that many other readers would, too. Television had also reported the demonstrations.

The report, by our Jerusalem correspondent and two other staff journalists, was not illustrated but it ran across six columns at the foot of an inside page on September 12 beneath the headline 'Palestinian joy – global condemnation'. It started: 'Palestinian gunmen at refugee camps in Lebanon fired into the air in celebration yesterday as the rest of the world united in revulsion at the "monstrous" and "abhorrent" attacks in the US.' We quoted a gunman firing celebratory rifle rounds in Jenin refugee camp on the West Bank: 'This is God's revenge for America's support of Israel.' We then reported Yasser Arafat's condemnation of the attacks and sorrow for the victims.

Correspondence with the reader in Israel, who had complained of the omission of any reference to this in the recent report, continued after publication of the 'correction'. He complained that I had not responded to his request to make it clear that the Palestinian demonstrations that were so like those of the Israelis had been organised by Yasser Arafat.

Meanwhile, two or three people had complained about anti-Palestinian bias in the 'correction' – in other words I was accused of unfairly favouring the Israeli complainant.

Last week a columnist in G2 suggested that two men convicted of a racial offence and each sentenced to 18 months in prison may not have been fairly treated. In particular he suggested that one of the two had simply been a bystander. As a reader pointed out in a letter to the editor, he omitted to say that the court had heard that this person had driven his car at a black police officer.

An argument has to survive consideration of salient facts. We usually recognise and include them, but not always.

September 16 2002

Matters of opinion

Editing the comment pages is probably one of the more coveted jobs on the paper. It gives the holder the opportunity and the heavy responsibility not simply of mediating the debate on the main issues of the day, but to some extent of stimulating it and moving it forward.

It is a civilising forum where people of strongly opposing views may speak their piece. However, hostilities do sometimes break out and the comment editor is berated for what are seen as sins both of inclusion and exclusion. 'When did you last carry a pro-Israel piece?' a reader asks (the answer is: quite recently). 'Why was George Galloway given space to defend himself [against the threat of expulsion from the Labour party over aspects of his anti-war position]?' 'Why waste space on Charles Krauthammer?' Krauthammer, a conservative Pulitzer prize-winning Washington Post columnist, had suggested, to put it crudely, that George Bush should raise the fingers of scorn to the United Nations.

The readers – the last two anyway – seem to me to be missing the point. The comment pages can reflect the Guardian ethos in two main ways. One is in columnists, not only its own, who address readers in the tone of liberal rationality that one hopes is associated with the paper. The other is in spanning the range of voices in a debate, including those in conflict with the paper's editorial line. The deputy editor said, 'The pages have a mission to bring you the kind of views that challenge you and give you a breadth of argument you won't find elsewhere. They explore issues that are always multi-dimensional.'

One of the things this section of the paper has been doing very effectively in the past couple of days is to pour cold water on the euphoria over the early military success of the war in Iraq. Yesterday's pages contained a piece by a former special adviser to the Foreign Office, the content of which is expressed in the headlines: 'This pyrrhic victory on the Tigris' and 'The outcome was never in doubt but the aftermath looks ominous.'

Elsewhere on the pages, one of the Guardian's senior foreign commentators was looking, not optimistically, at the implications of the war in the Gulf for the United States' future relations with the Muslim world. Another commentator was anticipating, with a conspicuous lack of enthusiasm, the extension of the McDonald's empire. 'Surely the Iraqis have suffered enough?' he concluded.

The previous day the comment editor's own column appeared. The headline and introduction read: 'The crudely colonial nature of this enterprise can no longer be disguised. Iraqis have paid the blood price for a fraudulent war.' Running alongside was a piece by the prime minister, not about the war, but about the baby bond provision of the budget.

The person editing these pages can always rely on a bumpy ride (the same thing might be said of their readers). The turbulence is even greater during a war. Recently a cut in an article by Bill Clinton, supporting Tony Blair's position on the Iraq war and timed for publication on the day of the Commons debate, proved controversial. The piece lost, among other trimmings, an exhortation to Labour MPs to support their leader. The general drift of the piece, and indeed the appeal to the British people to support Mr Blair, were not affected, but was it not of interest to readers that a former president of the US was prepared to make a direct appeal to British MPs? In my view the answer is: yes, of course it was.

So what happened? Was the cut a casualty of customary turmoil, the chaos factor that should never be underestimated in the context of newspapers? The comment editor says, yes, the piece came in very late and overlong, small cuts were made and normally they would have been referred back to the author, but they were made against the deadline.

I mention it as an indication of the kind of scrutiny these pages and those editing them get. It is probably true that the pages run by the present comment editor have represented a wider ranging debate than is available in any other English-language newspaper. The inclusion of Muslim writers and commentators from the Arab world is hugely appreciated, not least by US readers who lament the absence of this kind of thing in their own press.

One of the criticisms – itself arguable – is that the pages represent the extremities of argument well, but neglect the middle ground. Exceptions can be found, but the comment editors argue that power, in the US anyway, is not in the middle, not now at any rate.

The slogan of the comment pages should be, and perhaps it is: there's no pleasing everybody.

April 12 2003

Osama bin Laden in the Guardian

On Tuesday this week, January 6, the Guardian published a translated extract from the latest tape purporting to be from Osama bin Laden. It was presented under his byline on the first comment and analysis page of the paper, with the headline Resist the new Rome.

In presentation it differed in no way from any other piece occupying that slot. At the end there was a note that said: 'This is an edited extract of a recording believed to have been made by the al-Qaida leader, transmitted by al-Jazeera and translated by the BBC Monitoring Service.'

In fact, it was an edited version, reduced by more than half, of the 14 minutes of the tape broadcast by the Qatar-based satellite television station al-Jazeera. Al-Jazeera had taken that from the complete 47-minute tape, something that had been explained in a front-page story the previous day.

The extract was not trailed on the front page of the paper. It was not mentioned in the page 2 index. There was no cross-reference to it from the news pages. There was no editorial explaining why the paper had decided to carry it.

If the effect of encountering the byline on the comment pages was startling, it was perhaps even more so on the home page of the Guardian website, where, among the columnists listed under 'Today's comment', the name Osama bin Laden appeared with George Monbiot, Jackie Ashley, Zoe Williams and others.

Readers appear to have accepted the decisions both to carry the extract and to run it on the comment pages. As I write (midday Thursday), no reader has been in touch with me to register any objection to it, either its presence or position in the paper. Most of the dozen or so who wrote letters to the editor, four of which were published the following day, confined themselves to sardonic comments welcoming Bin Laden to the ranks of Guardian columnists, with one or two noting how well he fitted in.

There was, however, a vigorous discussion inside the paper, at the editor's morning conference on the day of publication, with several people speaking strongly against the decision to carry the extract on the comment pages.

I did not attend the editor's conference. However, the debate seemed to me one worth continuing. Later that day I sent to all journalists and editorial support staff an email inviting replies to these questions: '1. Was the Guardian right to run the piece? 2. Was it right to run it on a comment page? 3. If you say yes to 2, was it adequately introduced/presented?'

Exactly 150 people had replied by midday on Thursday: 142 thought the paper was right to publish the extract, eight thought the paper was wrong, one calling it 'appalling judgment', another saying that to suggest Bin Laden's 'ravings' were worthy of note was to demean Muslims; 67 thought it was right to run it on the comment pages, 83 thought it wrong; 39 of those who felt it was all right there thought the way it was presented inadequate; 26 thought it was fine on all counts.

Among the objections to its presence on the comment pages were the following: 'It was an incitement to murder – it was also an incitement to hatred on racial/religious grounds.' '[The position] gave it too much prominence and associated Bin Laden too much with the Guardian.' '[Bin Laden] forsook the arena of debate when he took up murder as a policy and he has no right to be there.' The question raised was, if a terrorist is given this kind of free access to the platform then where are the limits, or are there none?

Three senior journalists closely concerned in reporting and commenting on international affairs were among those strongly supporting the decision to run it on the comment pages. Here are some of their reasons: 'It is an interesting and significant statement.' 'It gives a terrific insight into the workings of the mind of the (US-declared) world enemy number one ... Most will feel better informed about the menace and motivations [of] al-Qaida.'

One said, 'We are living in a moment when the security services claim we are all at risk of another mega terrorist attack, and sky marshals on planes are vital. To hear what the arch-terrorist says is vital ... Giving someone space does not mean we endorse their views.'

By placing the extract on the comment pages, the paper was saying it was worthy of special attention – and so it was. It might have been presented differently, with the explanation of the source at the top rather than the bottom, for instance. Readers, however, appeared to have had no problem with it, and neither did I.

Ian Mayes was an editor on the comment pages 1991-92

January 10 2004

A justified complaint about an indefensible headline

Among my recent emails was one from Haifa in Israel which came quickly to the point: 'Sir, the Guardian is liar of the month in April 2004 at Take-a-Pen.' Take-a-Pen, I discovered, is a lobby group founded by Endre Mozes in late 2000. He set it up to try to counter the effects of the adverse media coverage Israel was receiving after the beginning of the second intifada, or Palestinian uprising.

In his email to me Mr Mozes explained that it was a headline in Guardian International, the edition of the paper that he read during a week in Paris, that attracted his attention. It read: 'Hungary foils "Jewish" terror plot.'

On his website, he reproduces the headline and part of the page of April 14 on which it appeared, with this introduction: 'On April 13, the Hungarian police arrested three Arabs suspected of planning to attack a Jewish museum in Budapest. The editor of the printed version of the Guardian international edition ... Nick Thorpe, writes that a "Jewish" terror plot was foiled.'

Mr Mozes' email also copied to me a letter from Maurice Ostroff, said to have been sent to the Guardian earlier. It had not reached me. All my correspondence is logged and I have been unable to find any trace of it. The letter says: 'My first reaction on reading the bold headline "Hungary foils 'Jewish' terror plot" ... was increased resentment against those troublesome Jews now plotting terror attacks in Hungary. Only after reading the entire article did I realise that the headline was completely misleading. The plot was not by Jews but against Jews. A typical case of the victim misrepresented as the culprit. Admittedly, on re-reading the headline, I became aware of the quotation marks surrounding the word Jewish.'

To pause for a moment here – Nick Thorpe is not the editor of the international edition. He did not write the headline. He is the journalist who filed the report from Budapest. Nowhere in it were the events he described referred to as a Jewish terror plot. I find it hard to believe that Mr Ostroff had to read the entire article to realise that the headline was misleading. Nick Thorpe's first paragraph says: 'A possible plot to blow up a new Holocaust museum in Budapest appeared to have been foiled yesterday when detectives arrested three men, a Palestinian and two Syrians, on suspicion of planning an attack.' That appears to me to resolve immediately any ambiguity in the headline.

Mr Ostroff's email continues: 'I believe you will agree that: (a) headlines have a major influence on readers' impressions – a great number of readers skim their newspaper headlines without reading the entire articles; (b) this headline creates the definite impression that a plot by Jews, not against Jews, has been foiled; (c) few readers would have paid attention to the quotation marks around the word "Jewish" and even for those who did notice them, the significance is unclear.'

We have covered this ground before, when the word 'massacre' appeared in quotation marks in a headline about Jenin. On that occasion it was supported by remarks by a Palestinian quoted in the accompanying report. On the present occasion the headline appeared to be saying exactly the opposite of what the text of the story said.

I agree with almost everything Mr Ostroff said in the second part of his email, quoted above. The headline is indefensible and should not have appeared. I would have come to that conclusion had Mr Ostroff's email reached me earlier. In the circumstances it would be churlish to complain about the overstated presentation on the Take-a-Pen website, which monitors and comments upon media coverage in 15 languages. But, 'liar'?

The headline to which the website rightly objected appeared only in the international edition. It did not appear in any edition of the Guardian printed in the United Kingdom. It did not appear on any report on the Guardian's own website.

The headline was not written by anyone on the staff of Guardian International. It was written by a subeditor for the main paper but changed after the page had been sent on to the next stage before publication. The page was withdrawn and a new version was then sent with the headline: Hungarian police foil terror plot. This is the headline you will find on the Guardian website. Guardian International, working at maximum pressure near its early deadline, picked up and printed the earlier page. It had no warning that a significant revision had been made. Until the system is improved it will remain a recipe for disaster. This time, with a little goodwill, some of the damage may be repaired.

May 29 2004

The Guardian and Israel in context

Here is a recent exchange of correspondence, of a kind familiar to all journalists involved in coverage of the Middle East. It dates from about a month ago: 'This morning's Palestinian attack on an Israeli [nursery] school is not even mentioned on the Guardian's website. Had a Palestinian child been killed while Israel went after a terrorist leader it would have been the Guardian's lead story. Your anti-semitic stance is thinly masked by your claims of liberalism.'

I replied: 'Dear T, What are you talking about? The story you refer to ran at the top of a page in our international news section in all editions of today's Guardian. It is a long dispatch from Chris McGreal in Jerusalem. The headline said, "Gaza braced for revenge after Hamas kills boy, 3". The same story with the same headline has been on the website all day.' I complained to him of his 'loose way with charges of anti-semitism'.

He came back: 'Ian, The Guardian's reporting about Israel has been consistently and hugely disproportionate. If the Israelis fired missiles at a Palestinian [nursery] school or shot a pregnant woman and her three daughters in the head at point blank range, it would be a big story featured prominently on the Guardian's website for days ... I spend half my time in the UK and understand that thinly veiled anti-semitism is a common cultural phenomenon, but that is no excuse. It is time for the Guardian to hold Islamic countries to the same standards of conduct as you hold Israel, the US and the UK.'

At the end of May I wrote a column responding to an email from Endre Mozes of Haifa in Israel, who runs a website and lobby group called Take-a-Pen. He complained of a headline, 'Hungary foils "Jewish" terror plot', which had been published in the international edition of the Guardian. What the Hungarian police had foiled, in fact, was a suspected plan to attack a Jewish museum in Budapest. I concluded it was a justified complaint about an indefensible headline.

This made me friends in some places but not in others. Mr Mozes has a page on his website called 'The Guardian watch & dialogue'. On it he acknowledges our 'friendly discussion' and explains that 'as a result of [my] positive intervention we have renamed this section not only a "Watch" but also a "Dialogue".'

I received this email, dispatched at breakfast time on the Saturday the column appeared: 'Your grovelling apology to the Jewish lobby is pathetically embarrassing. If it had been a video you would most certainly have been prostrate on the floor. And then to cap it off, you advertise a virulently anti-Palestinian website. It was only an inappropriate headline for God's sake. They happen all the time. I find it inconceivable that you would give such an abject apology to Palestinian people under any circumstances.'

At the end of her recent book, Disenchantment: The Guardian and Israel (Guardian Books, 2004), Daphna Baram – who is an Israeli journalist, a fellow of the Reuters Foundation and a senior associate member of St Antony's, Oxford – says: 'I was stunned by the amount of time, energy and thinking which everybody involved in Israel's coverage in the Guardian put into the task of getting it right.'

I wish I could place a copy of her book in the hands of everyone engaged or provoked by the Guardian's coverage (it would have a large circulation). Baram is excellent on the historical context, including the crucial friendship between the Guardian editor CP Scott and the Zionist leader Chaim Weizmann – a friendship that led to the Balfour declaration, which opened the way to the foundation of Israel.

An Israeli government official to whom the Guardian's involvement in the Balfour Declaration appeared to come as a surprise said to the paper's diplomatic editor recently: 'Ah, so that's why the Guardian dislikes Israel so much – guilt over its part in the Balfour declaration.'

Baram says in the preface to her book: 'Some readers may expect [me] to clarify the question of whether the Guardian is an anti-semitic newspaper. I can unburden you from any further reading by saying straight away: it is not. The allegation is offensive and lacks any basis. A more interesting question is whether it is an anti-Zionist newspaper, and, again, and somewhat to my surprise, I discovered that it is most certainly not.'

July 31 2004

Charges of an anti-Israel hoax
in south Lebanon

On Tuesday July 25 2006 the Guardian carried a report from south Lebanon headed: Red Cross ambulances destroyed in Israeli air strike on rescue mission. It appeared on page 6, the last of three pages devoted to the Middle East crisis that day. The report was filed from the southern Lebanon city of Tyre by one of the paper's most experienced foreign correspondents, a former Jerusalem correspondent, Suzanne Goldenberg.

She reported: 'Even in a war which has turned the roads of south Lebanon into killing zones, Israel's rocket strike on two clearly marked Red Cross ambulances on Sunday night set a deadly new milestone.'

Her report was compiled from information provided on the morning after the incident by the Red Cross in Tyre and from interviews with ambulance workers and others in hospital who said they had been injured in the attack. The ambulances were seen by the Guardian's staff photographer, Sean Smith, on July 25 (the day the Guardian report of the incident was actually published). He was able to see them before they were removed from the site where the attack was said to have taken place. Smith, who now has considerable experience in war zones, remains in no doubt that the ambulances had been subjected to a recent attack consistent with what had been reported.

Much the same story was carried by major news outlets around the world. But was it true? A California-based website poses the question: 'Could it be that the entire incident is a fabrication? All signs point to "yes".' You can read the entire argument leading to that conclusion at www.zombietime.com. This has been adopted by the pro-Israeli lobby Honest-Reporting, which asks: 'Why has the mainstream media not reported this hoax and admitted its mistake?' It then calls upon its subscribers to ask the same question of the following media outlets - a list which gives some idea of the extent of the coverage: Associated Press, ITN, Time magazine, the Boston Globe, the Age in Australia, NBC News, the New York Times and the Guardian.

I have received a number of emails referring to the Zombie-time website, one from a reader describing his complaint as 'purely personal', concluding, 'Before I take this complaint forward to the Press Complaints Commission I would appreciate your comments on the linked website [Zombietime] and also whether you intend to retract the story.' On the basis of my inquiries over several days last week I do not intend to suggest that the paper should retract its report.

Two Australian newspapers, in fact, revisited the story after the country's foreign minister, Alexander Downer, accused some of the world's 'most prestigious media' of falling for a hoax. One of them, the Australian, carried its rebuttal under the heading, 'Downer's unfounded faith in the internet', and it accused him of being hoaxed by what it called 'a callous blog' (Zombietime is a website not a blog). The heading on the Age story speaks for itself: 'Ambulance attack evidence stands the test'.

What the Zombietime website, which takes issue with both of these Australian rebuttals, does show is a fairly large number of inconsistencies and anomalies in the reporting and pictorial coverage of the event across the media: whether these are larger in number than might normally be expected to occur in reporting from a war zone is a matter for conjecture. A Guardian picture archivist with a special interest in images from areas of conflict, who carried out extensive research for me, concluded that there was cause for doubt about the nature of the munitions involved and the manner of their delivery, but not in the reality of the attack. Suzanne Goldenberg told me: 'I remain confident that the story was true.' She points out that she and Sean Smith reported the story first hand and independently and did not rely on what purported to be amateur video footage of the incident.

An Israeli military spokesman in a statement to the Guardian said, 'This was in a very dangerous area ... from which 150 rockets had been fired before that date. We had advised the civilian populations and other organisations like the UN and the Red Cross that it was a dangerous area and any movement had to be coordinated with the Israeli army. We don't know for sure if those two ambulances were hit by Israeli fire. We cannot confirm or not confirm.

'All we know is that we don't know of any incident when Israeli missiles would have hit a vehicle marked as being a vehicle from the Red Cross. We don't recognise hitting any Red Cross vehicles on that date in particular.'

Roland Benjamin-Huguenin, the UK spokesperson for the International Committee of the Red Cross (ICRC), joined the organisation in 1983, visiting prisoner of war camps set up in south Lebanon by Israeli forces after the invasion of 1982. He was in south Lebanon throughout the present conflict. He said he and other ICRC delegates had worked daily alongside the volunteers of the Lebanese Red Cross in Tyre and elsewhere in Lebanon. He had seen the ambulances and saw no reason to question that they had been subjected to an attack. He told me that the Red Cross 'categorically rejects and denies' the version being circulated on the internet.

The Zombietime version invites the conclusion that the Lebanese Red Cross conspired in an elaborate anti-Israel propaganda plot to dupe the world's media. I do not think that is proven at all.

September 11 2006

Fact, figures and terms of reference in the Middle East

The Guardian's coverage of the Middle East has been questioned on two particular points this week. One is its reporting of the release by Israel of 339 Palestinian prisoners (the Israeli figure as I write is 334). The other is the name used for the structure being erected by the Israelis across Israeli and Palestinian territory and called by Israel the 'security fence'.

On the first point, the Guardian is criticised for reporting, on August 5, this remark by Yasser Arafat, the Palestinian president: 'They say they are going to release 400, and then they turn around and arrest 800', and the comment by the correspondent that 'Hundreds more have been arrested in the meantime.' This has excited the attention of the pro-Israeli lobby Honest Reporting, whose followers poured hundreds of emails into the letters queue this week.

They were responding to an email communique that concluded: 'Honest Reporting encourages readers to challenge the Guardian to provide evidence for its claim that "hundreds" of Palestinians have recently been arrested – a claim used by the Guardian to downplay, in cynical fashion, the significance of Israel's large-scale prisoner release.'

The paper was chastised in many emails for a report of August 7, headed 'Joy and anger as Israel frees 339', in which its correspondent said, 'the Israelis have arrested almost as many Palestinians since the beginning of the ceasefire five weeks ago.'

This appears to me to be a perfectly defensible statement. Our Jerusalem correspondent was told by the Israeli army that it had arrested 237 'wanted Palestinians' since the declaration of the ceasefire on June 29, of whom 72 were arrested in the first week of August.

He says that this total is solely for Palestinians who were on the army's wanted lists and who remain in custody. It does not include Palestinians arrested, for example, for stone throwing, or those arrested and still held for failing to have the necessary passes, or those detained by the police.

Only the Palestinian leadership is talking of a figure of 600-800 arrests. The liberal Israeli newspaper Haaretz has said that 'an examination of the records since the ceasefire was declared on June 29 shows that the army has arrested nearly as many Palestinians since then – 320 – as the number it freed on Wednesday.'

In the absence of definitive figures it seems to me that the Guardian, through its correspondent, has erred on the side of caution.

To turn to the 'security fence'. A spokeswoman for the Israeli embassy in London said: 'Over the past 30 months, a sustained campaign of Palestinian terror attacks has killed more than 800 Israelis and injured many more thousands in more than 18,000 terror attacks ... A security fence is being constructed in order to impede the terrorists' access to Israel. This measure is being taken to save lives and not to annex territory.

'The first stage of construction, completed last week, measures 115 km (approximately 71 miles) ...The fence, which will be between 50 and 70 metres wide, will be enhanced with hi-tech equipment to prevent infiltration into Israel. Underground and long-range sensors, unmanned aerial vehicles, trenches, landmines and guard paths would all be used to prevent terrorists from infiltrating into Israel.'

She added: 'It is important to note that this fence has no ideological or political significance. Its only rationale is to prevent terror attacks against Israeli civilians, and the physical route is determined solely by Israel's security needs ... After almost three years of Palestinian terror, the fence is the only way for Israel to defend its people and to reduce the intolerable price in blood that has been paid with the lives of innocent Israelis ...'

The Palestinians call it the apartheid wall. It is also called the Berlin wall, the dividing wall, the separation wall. The fact is, it is a wall in some sections and a fence in others. The headline on a long discussion of the terminology by the pro-Palestinian website Electronic Intifada (electronicintifada.net/v2/article1775.shtml) seems to state the reality fairly: 'Is it a fence? Is it a wall? No, it's a separation barrier.'

Finding terminology that favours neither one view nor the other is not easy. The Guardian approach is to quote the term 'security fence' and to attribute it to the Israelis. The paper's Jerusalem correspondent also tends to refer to it as a 'fence and wall', or sometimes 'barrier'. The latter, for something the size of a motorway, seems closer to the mark.

Additional research: Isabelle Chevallot.

August 9 2003

8.

IMAGES OF BRUTALITY & TRAUMA

Television and in recent years the internet have greatly increased the expectation that news reports of the most challenging events in the world will be reported, in pictures as well as in words, in unflinching detail. Judgments in this area for both the journalist and the reader involve but almost always go beyond questions of taste. If readers do not think they have been taken close enough to the reality of war then they will accuse the paper of sanitising. If they think the paper has taken them too close they will accuse it of cynically seeking to shock in an effort to boost circulation. Some of the complexities involved in specific decisions to use strong images in widely differing contexts are discussed in these columns, once again quite often raising questions that are left unanswered.

Several of the pieces consider the use of photographs of dead people. One is concerned with a picture of a naked Iraqi prisoner in Abu Ghraib. Should the Guardian have masked his face? In not doing that did it, while presenting a picture of a man stripped of his dignity, play some small part in his humiliation itself? These are just two of the questions readers asked. In one column the question was not only whether a shocking image - the severed face of a small girl – should have been used but whether it should, in any case, have been used to illustrate a television column (it related to a programme about face transplants), where it somehow seemed doubly shocking?

I have written a great many columns about the use of pictures (there are more later in this book). From the reaction to them it was clear that readers quite often had simply not thought that these matters were seriously considered before publication. In the vast majority of cases I looked at that was not the case. The decisions in the end, of course, may remain a matter for argument.

Northern Ireland: troubles on the front page

On Monday this week the Guardian's front page, carrying the headline 'Terror threat to Ulster peace', was dominated by a photograph of the murdered loyalist leader, Billy Wright, surrounded by four khaki-clad, masked members of the Loyalist Volunteer Force, three of whom held hand-guns. The full-frontal, uncompromising presentation of the picture prompted protests from a number of readers – no more than half a dozen so far as I can ascertain – who felt the paper had wrongly allowed itself to be used for terrorist propaganda and might, in the process, have been exacerbating an already inflammatory situation.

I'll return to the complaints in a moment. But, first of all, how did the picture come to be taken? The photographer who took it, and who has spent all his working life in Northern Ireland, was in Portadown on Sunday evening waiting for the body of Billy Wright to be returned to his home ahead of the funeral.

'I went down to the Brownstown area of Portadown and parked near the cul-de-sac where Wright had lived. It was already dark, and raining. There were small groups of people standing around with a group of four or five who looked like absolute thugs more or less sealing off the street. One of them came over and asked what I was doing. I said I was a freelance and hoped to get a picture of Wright's remains being returned to his home. I was told the body had arrived half an hour earlier.

'They went into another huddle and then one came across and said, "Come with me." I felt a bit uneasy because I was the only camera around. I was left for about 15 minutes sheltering from the rain in the porch of Wright's house at the end of the cul-de-sac.

'The guy who had led me to the house returned and said, "OK, come in." I was drawn towards the living room. I was stopped by this fellow who said, "No, you're upstairs." As soon as I got to the landing I was conscious of the open door of the front bedroom and the coffin and khaki-clad figures. No one followed me in.

'Because I'd come in from the cold and wet, my lens kept steaming up. A couple of times I had to say hang on while I wiped it. I was conscious of the Lenin-like appearance of Wright's body, which a lot of people have remarked on since seeing the pictures. I shot about 30 frames. Then a voice from the landing said, "Right lads, put the gear on the ground and salute." They put their guns down, turned towards the body and saluted. One then read a short statement and I left.

'I went back to the hotel in Portadown and got the pictures out. It was already late, nearly 8pm, by the time I sent the Guardian's picture [transmitted electronically down a telephone line].' The duty editor on Sunday evening, remote from the sweaty-palmed experience of the photographer, had, on the earlier promise of a picture, decided to wait as long as he could. By the time the picture was actually available to him there was very little time for deliberation. There was a discussion around the desk, lasting for five to 10 minutes.

It was clearly a very powerful picture. The developments in Northern Ireland were thought to constitute the most important story of the moment. The slaughter of chickens in Hong Kong, one of the possible options for the front, was briefly reconsidered but it was decided to stand by an earlier decision to carry it on page 2. Beyond that, there was little contending for the lead on page 1.

The body of the dead loyalist, the gunmen around the body, were considered to provide a chilling image totally appropriate to shocking events which challenged the peace process. This reading of it, the duty editor felt, was endorsed, and encouraged in others, by the words of the Northern Ireland secretary, Mo Mowlam, which were carried alongside the picture. They included, 'Everyone has been well aware that splinter groups are an ever-present threat to the current peace.' One thing the editor regretted was not having, in the caption, spelled out the staged nature of the picture. Others felt that this spoke for itself. It was also felt that if the Loyalist Volunteer Force regarded it as propaganda, it was unlikely to work in the way intended. And while the picture was recognised as a cliche, it was thought that the circumstances surrounding it placed it in a special category.

To return to the complaints. One person to whom I spoke thought that it was a violent image of a kind the paper should not be printing in any case. Beyond that – and this was a view shared by all those who rang – she felt that the paper had colluded with terrorists seeking publicity and in so doing had demeaned itself and its readers.

I believe the paper was justified both in using it, and in displaying it in the way that it did. To have had the picture available, to have apprehended the consequences that might flow from the event it addressed, and not to have used it, would perhaps have been chicken.

January 3 1998

Abu Ghraib: the face of abuse unmasked

A picture carried across five columns on the front page of the Guardian on May 10 2004 had this descriptive caption: 'A naked Iraqi prisoner cowers in front of barking dogs held by US soldiers in Abu Ghraib jail.'

A number of readers questioned the way the picture had been presented and a few said the Guardian should not have used it at all. The paper has carried more than 15 different pictures of prisoners in Abu Ghraib since it published the first on its front page on April 30 – a hooded figure with wires attached, standing on a box.

What was different about this one? Unlike almost all of those used earlier, in which the heads of the prisoners had been hooded by their guards, the face of this man was quite clearly visible. He would probably have been recognisable to those who knew him. He would certainly recognise himself.

One reader wrote: 'Please could you explain to me how the photo of a naked Iraqi prisoner on your front page does not infringe his human rights?' A reader of the online edition, writing from Germany, said: 'Please, please replace the image of the naked Iraqi on your front page and world news page with something less upsetting. It is shameful enough that he has been abused in such a way, but for you to broadcast his humiliation to all your online readers worldwide is certainly adding insult to injury.'

Although readers did not always say so, it seemed to be the fact that the man's face was shown that increased the degree of distress communicated by the picture. 'I realise that you have printed such pictures before on this terrible subject and I know that it is important for us to receive this information,' one wrote. 'Nevertheless, I object to [this picture] because I feel it is now bordering on voyeurism – it feels like incitement, somehow, or as if we all have a part of this man's shame and humiliation. I do not wish to be in any way associated with this sort of inhumanity, and by blazoning it on the front page of the paper it makes us all implicated.'

There is, I suggest, some confusion here between the crime and evidence of the crime. Publication of the photograph does not infringe the man's human rights; but it does graphically convey an infringement of his rights. Taken with other photographs, and we now know there are at least 1,800, many showing greater abuses, the picture has an imperative that demands prominent publication – and demands it, apparently, regardless of all consequences (for instance the further excitement of anti-American feeling in the Arab world). The story has been rightly persistent.

All right, one reader said, but 'why didn't you use a black box to cover the naked prisoner's eyes – as convention demands of civilised societies – in order to give him a certain degree of respect, masking his identity, while still getting the story across?'

A glance across the other British newspapers reveals the confusion – or let us call it differences of opinion – on this. Some pixelated (electronically masked) the prisoner's face. Others did not.

You might ask yourself the question: 'If this had been done to me would I want the world to know about it – would I want the world to know it had been done specifically to me?' To put it another way: 'Would I, given all the efforts of the perpetrators of these abuses to ensure the anonymity of their victims, want to be consigned to anonymity by a newspaper which had had the opportunity to get me out of it?'

In fact, as the Guardian reported on Thursday this week, prisoners who, despite the hoods placed over their heads, have been able to recognise themselves in these photographs are now beginning to come forward to identify themselves and to testify to their maltreatment.

The editor of the Guardian strongly defends the decision to carry the picture as it was received by the paper and not to mask the face. He feels the paper made a mistake at the beginning of the Iraq war when, after a request from the Ministry of Defence, it pixelated the face of an Iraqi soldier who had surrendered to US marines. He said that to have continued to do that, or to do it systematically, would change the face of war reporting.

We do not know what the particular prisoner in the picture had done or was alleged to have done. Would it, should it, make any difference? Who is diminished by the revelation of such an abuse, the prisoner, his guards, or, as the reader I quoted earlier seemed to sense, all of us? Was it more or less uncomfortable because we were asked to look the prisoner in the face?

May 15 2004

Attack on London: distress in the detail

Amid general praise for the Guardian's coverage of the bombings in London there has been some strong criticism of three things in particular. One was a photograph across the top of page 2 on Friday (the day after the attacks) showing 'a blackened and bloodied passenger' on a trolley being treated by paramedics.

Another was a picture used on Saturday, also across the full width of an inside page, showing surviving passengers on the roofless upper deck of the bus in Tavistock Square. The head and shoulders of one, or possibly two, of the victims, presumably dead, were discernible at the back of the bus where the bomb went off.

The third cause for complaint was a first-person account – a 'harrowing account', the introduction warned – by a sergeant of the British Transport Police describing the carnage at the site of the bomb between King's Cross and Russell Square. That was carried on the front page on Saturday.

To look at this first: a reader wrote, 'I question the Guardian's judgment in publishing such a distressingly graphic account of the appalling injuries suffered … A university friend of mine is missing … I will always wonder if the woman without limbs who could not be helped was my missing friend.'

There should have been a stronger warning about the content. However, I think the Guardian was right to use it, to allow the rescuer to say that is what it was really like, and to share his experience – running it on the front page practically suggested a duty to listen to him. He ended by describing his ascent to daylight: 'I stood there, I felt lonelier than I thought was possible.'

Were the reasons for using it, the need to tell and to know, the desire to stand with the person who had gone to help, strong enough to override the likelihood of adding to the distress of friends and relatives of those missing? It is a difficult question to answer 'yes' to, but that in effect is what the paper did.

Three of those who objected to the picture of the man on the trolley were doctors. They objected particularly because it intruded upon an attempt to resuscitate the man. One accused the Guardian of 'an uncharacteristic lapse of taste', another of 'gross insensitivity'.

This picture was taken from a television sequence shown by the BBC, which responded to complaints by saying the footage should not have been broadcast and that it regretted doing so. The Guardian does not know the identity of the man. It does not know if he has survived.

I sent a note round to all editorial staff with the complete letter of complaint from one of the doctors, and one of the emails, also complete, complaining about the picture of the bus. I asked the question: Were we right to use these pictures?

The great majority, in the case of the man on the trolley, agreed with the doctors and thought the paper was wrong to publish the picture. One issue was identity. It was felt that the possibility that the man would be recognised increased the intrusion. The degree to which his face was revealed in the greatly enlarged printed version seemed to surprise those who took the decision to use it; otherwise they might have decided to mask the face, making it clear that this had been done. This picture was used on Friday – before the paper became aware of the objections to the BBC – when it seemed to express both the horror of what had happened and the nature of the task in which the emergency services were engaged.

The objections to the bus picture arose from the detectable presence of the victims at the rear of the bus rather than any possibility of recognition, which was slight or nonexistent. Nevertheless, some of the newspapers that used this picture erased or blurred that part of the image. Others did not, among them the Guardian, which has a policy not to manipulate pictures – or not to manipulate pictures without saying it has done so.

Fewer journalists shared the objections to this picture. Some thought the use of both pictures showed the paper was prepared to apply the same criteria to its coverage of such an event inside the UK as anywhere else in the world.

In the middle of Wednesday afternoon, one journalist answering the question of whether the bus picture should have been used, said no. He had just learned a friend had been among those killed on it. He is not alone here in suffering loss.

None of these decisions, the right ones or the wrong ones, have been taken in isolation: in these excruciatingly difficult areas we remain divided on which was which.

July 16 2005

A picture of a severed face

On May 6 2005, on page 18 of the daily tabloid second section G2, one of the paper's television critics reviewed a programme called Face Race, shown on the Discovery channel. To quote the review, the programme was about a 'little girl in northern India [who] had her ... face torn off by an agricultural machine' and about the apparently successful attempts of doctors to sew it back on. It also dealt with progress towards face transplants by surgeons in the US, 'inspired', it said, 'by the Indian girl's story'.

The review, under the heading 'Keeping up appearances', was illustrated with a picture of 'the child's face before being reattached', showing it 'in two pieces but complete with scalp and hair'. Almost the entire face, including her nose – the mask, so to speak – was shown in the picture, from the top of her head, complete with plait, down to her lower lip. It had been cleaned and was lying on a checked cloth, ready for the surgery to reattach it.

Two readers complained. One said: 'I was very distressed by the photograph on the TV pages ... of the remains of the face of a young girl following a horrific accident. This is the most harrowing picture I have ever seen in the Guardian, and it appeared in the most unlikely place. I find this unacceptable.' This reader also strongly disliked the tone of the review, finding it 'inappropriate given the sensitive subject matter, and an example of tabloid sensationalism'. I was asked to answer two questions: 'Is there a policy on matters like this, and, if so, do you believe that this policy has been infringed?'

The other reader expressed a similar view: 'I thought it was a serious mistake to use the photo of a child's torn-off face to illustrate [a] TV review ... I imagine that the TV programme ... may have given more context to it, but in isolation and in the "light" end of the paper, I didn't expect to be confronted with such a horrible image … It really did make me feel physically ill.'

When I asked how this particular picture came to be chosen as the illustration for the television review that day I was told it was the only one available. So was the choice to use it or not to use it? No, the format of the page demands the use of a picture so a picture, the picture, had to be used.

I am paraphrasing part of separate conversations I had with the page editor, the picture editor and the art director. Of course, the picture did not have to be used. A picture could have been chosen to illustrate the other programme included in the television review that day, a new sitcom on BBC2 called The Robinsons. To some extent that would run against the logic of the layout but it has been done from time to time in the past and could have been done on this occasion, as the art director pointed out.

The picture, whether or not it was used because of the requirements of the design, was in the end chosen because no reason was seen not to use it. It illustrated the review of a programme about an extraordinary surgical feat, and an extraordinary human story. It was not a case, I was assured, where ethical considerations were set aside for the sake of expediency.

Nevertheless, some interesting questions remain. Should the picture have been used at all? What purpose did the picture serve? Is the question of whether or not the picture should have been used simply one of taste, or does it go beyond that? Some time ago I wrote a column about a decision to manipulate electronically the image of a severed limb in a photograph of the immediate aftermath of a terrorist bombing in Madrid, so that it did not look like a limb at all. I said the paper was wrong to do that, or that if it felt it had good reasons for doing it then it should have said so at the time.

If the paper felt qualms about showing a picture of a severed arm or leg why did it not feel qualms about showing the severed face of a small girl? The approval of the girl's parents was required for making the television programme and presumably extended to the release of the publicity photograph. Did that make it all right to use the picture? Would the Guardian have used the picture if the small girl whose face was torn off had been British, or European, or white?

To return to the two questions asked by the first reader. There is no policy to cover such a case and therefore no policy was infringed. There should be a policy to ask ourselves a bit more rigorously these questions, some of which you have asked on our behalf.

May 21 2005

The column about the alteration of the Madrid bombing photograph originally appeared on March 20 2004 (reprinted here in Chapter 10)

Iraq: defining rules for images of war

One image in the Guardian's coverage of the war in Iraq disturbed readers more than any other. That was a two-column picture – used on the front page on April 2 – of the corpse of an Iraqi baby, killed in a US assault near the city of Babylon. One reader wrote: 'Is there no human dignity left in our media today? [This photograph] defies belief. It is absolutely outrageous that newspapers are allowed to get away with such utter disregard for human life and go against all standards of decency ...'

Another wrote: 'I understand the reasoning behind using strong imagery to convey the atrocities of war, but I feel very strongly that using this photograph was not right.' Surely, this reader asked, the graphic text and a larger photograph on the same page of a man grieving over the body of his mother (one of 15 members of his family, including six children, it was said, killed in the attack), were sufficient to establish the horror of what had happened?

She continued: 'I felt that I had looked on something that should have been private and found myself wanting to rail against the editor of the Guardian rather than those who caused the baby's death, which was surely not the intention.'

Another reader commented, '[This picture] raises the whole issue of the dignity of the child and its family ... did the editorial team not consider that when they published the article?'

Some of the objections came from within the paper. One advertising executive wrote: 'I feel that the picture was wholly inappropriate especially due to the complaints aimed at the al-Jazeera ... coverage of the war.' Many of the complaints reaching this colleague were that the picture was concealed below the fold on the front page and therefore, as another reader put it, provided no opportunity for parents to screen their children from it should they have wished to do that.

Exactly a week later the Guardian published on its front page another picture that shocked some readers. This was a six-column close-up photograph showing the bloodied legs and feet, including those of a small child, of corpses piled up in a mortuary in Baghdad, accompanied by a long contextual dispatch from the paper's correspondent.

A reader, who also referred to the picture of the dead baby, wrote: 'I wonder if you realise the obscenity in the relentless availability of such violent images of the dead victims. Is it ethical for you to serve this up on a plate to us for breakfast? ... These photos will not stop the war, and are used to create headlines and sell newspapers.'

These comments run counter to many others from readers who want to be told what is going on and are prepared to tolerate strong images provided their use is justified by the context. I paraphrase the comments of a US reader who seemed to sum up the feeling of many: If we can do it we can look at it.

I quote these comments because they seem highly relevant to the debate called for at a recent Media Guardian forum on war coverage by Mark Damazer, the deputy director of BBC News, to establish where the boundaries are drawn. He referred in particular to the pictures from al-Jazeera of two dead British soldiers, which were not shown by the BBC when they first became available but were shown (for eight seconds) with the faces pixelated (obscured) in a documentary two months later. The parents of the soldiers were among the great many who protested.

The Guardian, although the matter was considered at some length, did not use the pictures largely because of the high probability of recognition by relatives even, it was felt, with the faces obscured: only two soldiers were missing. Is that a valid reason for withholding pictures of British or US casualties when so many pictures of dead and injured Iraqis were appearing? One Guardian photographer said the army strongly discouraged the taking of pictures of British casualties, making it clear that in any case they were not to be identified.

Should pictures be withheld from publication when the same or similar images are freely circulated on the internet or on satellite television? That question will become more pressing.

July 5 2003

Victoria Climbie: a justified disturbance

The front page on Wednesday last week was dominated by a deep four-column close-up photograph of the murdered eight-year-old girl Victoria Climbie. It drew attention, uncompromisingly and unmissably, to the paper's coverage of the published report of the inquiry into her death conducted by Lord Laming.

The caption read: 'A photograph of Victoria Climbie, released by the inquiry, taken in July 1999 after she was admitted to a hospital casualty unit with scalding to her face and head. Released back into the care of her aunt [who with her boyfriend is now serving a life sentence for Victoria's murder], she was dead within seven months.'

The heading above the picture directly addressed this acutely distressing image. It said: 'There were 12 chances to save Victoria Climbie. This was one. Seven months later she was dead.' This was a line totally justified by the inquiry report, the paper's account of which, by its social affairs editor, ran in a single column alongside the picture before turning to an inside page. In the inquiry report Lord Laming and his colleagues condemned the failures of a string of agencies – social workers, police, NHS staff – who missed more than 12 opportunities, in fact, to save the girl.

Further reports by the social affairs editor and by the reporter who had followed the case through the trial at the Old Bailey two years ago, entirely occupied pages 8 and 9. In addition there was a leading article, which began: 'Even in the notoriously grim list of child abuse cases over the last 30 years, none has been more shocking than the murder of Victoria Climbie.'

The following email arrived on Wednesday afternoon: 'Some months ago, you published a picture of Victoria Climbie ... It was a shocking picture, made unnecessarily large to, I presume, emphasise the horror of her injuries. It had a very distressing effect on me personally, but I can see why you might have deemed it necessary. You have again today chosen to use a picture of a battered Victoria ... I hope this will be the last time you use Victoria in this way. While I am well aware that there is a major context to this usage, can I plead that this little girl, whose injuries were ignored by far too many people when she was alive, be allowed at least some dignity in her death, and not be the victim of future exploitation in this gratuitous "shock tactic" way?'

In fact, the front-page picture of Victoria had not been used in the Guardian before. The photograph to which the reader referred, a profile photograph of Victoria showing her injuries, was used on two occasions. The first was a two-column version used with a report during the course of the public inquiry, on page 15, September 29 2001. The second, the one which the reader had in mind, was used across several columns, the full depth of a tabloid spread, in a supplement, 'Ending child abuse deaths', produced by the Guardian in association with the National Society for the Prevention of Cruelty to Children and published with the paper's Society section on October 23 last year (the NSPCC has accepted responsibility for its share of the blame for Victoria's death and apologised to the Climbie family).

It is reasonable to assume that most readers did not see the use of the picture last week as gratuitous. The email I have quoted was one of only two complaints received by the evening of the day following publication. When the Guardian does something that is perceived as gratuitously shocking then complaints are sometimes counted in hundreds.

The deputy editor (news) said: 'I spent a long time over the decision whether to use the picture, thinking hard over the potential allegation that we were simply doing it to shock in a gratuitous way. [But] in the end there was the story of how this poor, unfortunate child had been failed on 12 occasions by police, social workers and NHS staff. Once I felt I had got the words right on the headline and the caption I was convinced we were doing the right thing [telling a tragic story] in a powerful and potentially enduring way.'

The reporter most involved in the coverage and the social affairs editor think as one on this. The latter said: 'The reader is right to be disturbed and we (and Lord Laming) were right to disturb her. [Lord Laming] was not "using" Victoria, and neither were we. The picture poses the basic question – how on earth did so many professionals miss so many signs that something was wrong?'

The reader is also right to question the paper's motives. However, on this occasion, and in this context, I think the Guardian got it right.

February 3 2003

Iraq: a closer view of death

A leader yesterday, 'What should we tell of the horror of war?', expressed the daily dilemma faced by journalists during the past week. The leader quoted the Times correspondent based with the British army during the Crimean war: 'Am I to tell these things, or hold my tongue?' – easy to answer so far as words are concerned, but more difficult when dealing with pictures, the 'far more troubling' images of war, as the leader put it.

One of the first emails I opened on Thursday morning was a message of congratulations for that day's front-page picture. The photograph was carried across six columns beneath the headline 'Wayward bombs bring marketplace carnage'. The caption read, 'The body of an Iraqi man caught in the Baghdad marketplace bombing is covered by a crowd of local people.' It was taken by Goran Tomasevic for Reuters.

The reader said it was not that anyone liked looking at appalling images – in this case of a clearly identifiable person – but he felt they were a corrective to the pictures that up to that point had come from the cameramen and photographers 'embedded' with the US and British forces.

Shortly afterwards I had an email expressing 'absolute disgust' at the paper's decision to publish the same photograph. 'I am amazed at your lack of sensitivity in publishing a photograph of a dead civilian, close up and in colour. I cannot imagine you would publish a similar picture in the aftermath of, say, a terrorist attack on London and I believe the same standards should apply no matter where the victim is located.' Several similar letters of protest followed.

From the paper's point of view the strong instinct, and you might say the pressure upon it from a large number of its readers, is to show the war as it is and not to collude in sanitising it through excessive caution in the way it is represented pictorially.

That means constantly testing the boundaries of acceptability. But how far should those boundaries be stretched?

Was the paper right or wrong, for example, to withhold from you some of the pictures that have been broadcast by al-Jazeera during the week?

One of these was a close-up of an Iraqi boy, clearly recognisable, killed by a bullet through the head, part of his skull still attached but lifted and laid alongside. This was not shown on the website and originally rejected for publication in the paper because of the extremely horrific nature of the image combined with a lack of contextual information – the who, where and when. However, a version of it did appear on Wednesday as one half of Steve Bell's political cartoon on the main comment page of the paper.

Steve Bell had no doubt at all that the photograph on which his drawing was based should have been published. Yesterday, in fact, it did get in, used quite small, illustrating with other images a report about the way in which Muslims in Britain were following the war. It was one of the pictures from al-Jazeera shown on the website of the Muslim Association of Britain.

The other pictures you were not shown by the Guardian were stills from a video supplied by an unknown source to al-Jazeera of the bodies of two dead British soldiers. There was a lengthy discussion over whether or not to use a cropped version of one of these, in which the soldier shown would not have been recognisable. But since only two soldiers were missing, the probability of recognition by relatives was high and this was felt to be an important factor. The question was: would the reasons for using a picture – the main one being a commitment to conveying war's reality – outweigh the reasons for not using it, the main one being the high probability of recognition?

The editor decided that the answer in this case was no and the picture was not used. That decision was taken shortly before the arrival of a request from the Ministry of Defence asking that none of those pictures should be used. 'At this stage we are not able to confirm whether or not [the soldiers in the pictures] are British,' it said.

On the day on which those pictures were absent from the paper, the Guardian carried not only the photograph of the dead Iraqi on the front, but a large picture of another dead Iraqi on page 3, and, on a later page, a picture of a British soldier, apparently grinning, holding 'an Iraqi captive near Basra'. A black colleague commented: 'My main worry is that we find it easier to publish pictures of dead black people, or non-whites, than we do dead white people.'

Yesterday's leader, in fact, asked: 'Is there something objectionable – even racist – in only showing Iraqi victims of war?' We have more questions than answers.

March 29 2003

9.

THE CHALLENGES OF THE INTERNET & NEW MEDIA

Some of the liveliest matters with which I have had to deal fall into this section, starting with the Guardian's own attempt in effect to influence the voters in a US swing state (what in the UK would be called a marginal) to register a vote against the Bush administration. The way in which, to do that, it exploited possibilities opened by the new media are described. Whether it was right to do that is a question that remains. A majority of Guardian journalists who responded to an internal poll I conducted thought it wrong. So did I.

The extraordinary influence that can be exercised through the internet and the speed with which information and misinformation can girdle the globe are illustrated here by the story, told in two columns, of the Guardian's erroneous report misquoting the then US deputy secretary of defence, Paul Wolfowitz. This report was not just in error. It was completely wrong and was removed from the website with a full explanation of why that was done.

Another column here refers to the removal from the website of an article dealing with an alleged plot to use the poison ricin in an attack on London. In this case no explanation was given for the removal, which was, in fact, for legal reasons concerning the identity of witnesses. After six months during which the legal requirements had been clarified and met the article was restored to the website, but not before various conspiracy theories had developed. In this case they were checked simply by explaining what had happened and why.

This section also includes a discussion on a matter not generally resolved: should some kind of statute of limitations apply to pejorative material that remains instantly available in the online archive? In this case we are talking about a negative restaurant review. We still rely on readers to note the date on the review and to decide themselves whether the opinions expressed are likely to remain relevant.

Here is a paradox. I have left out of this book a column, perhaps among my most widely read, dealing with the vexed problem of my resolution of a complaint from Noam Chomsky concerning the content and presentation of an interview with him. In my conclusion I substantially agreed with Professor Chomsky. This was then challenged in a formal complaint by others who said there had been nothing wrong with the content of the interview, that it should not have been corrected and that the Guardian and I should apologise to the journalist concerned. The matter was then referred to the external ombudsman of the Guardian, John Willis, who endorsed my conclusions although he felt my decision to remove the interview from the website had been unnecessary. I continue to believe that overall I came to the right conclusion, just as I am sure the people who objected to my conclusion continue to believe I was wrong. The whole matter is easily found in an electronic search for those interested enough to seek it. From the point of view of the journalist at the centre of all this, however, I feel that a system which I believe is fair can act unfairly over time through its live presence on the internet. I have imposed a kind of a statute of limitations on myself so far as references to the journalist by name are concerned, and similarly with one or two other cases in which the surrounding hubbub on the internet blew things, in my opinion, out of all proportion.

Dear Limey assholes

For more than a week the Guardian has been under an unprecedented email bombardment from the United States. The stimulus was an exercise mounted by G2, the tabloid second section of the paper, to put individual voters of undeclared party allegiance in the presidential election in Clark County, Ohio – narrowly balanced between Republicans and Democrats – in touch with individual Guardian readers.

The latter were urged to write 'citizen to citizen, explaining why this election matters to you, and which issues you think ought to matter to the US electorate'. The principle followed had earlier been expounded in a comment piece, under the heading 'US policy now affects every citizen on the planet. So we should all have a say in who gets to the White House'.

Although the G2 article did not presume to say which way it wanted the unaffiliated citizens of Clark County to vote, the front page of the main broadsheet that day carried the open declaration: 'What you can do to beat Bush – with a little help from the folks in Ohio'.

To facilitate its campaign, the Guardian obtained, on payment of a fee of $25, a copy of the file of voters for Clark County. It extracted from the 85,000 names on it the 36,000 with undeclared affiliation. It then arranged, through a special website, to provide readers with the address of an individual resident of Clark County.

The features editor of the Guardian, in a piece in G2 on Thursday, explained that in the few days that the site operated before it was hacked into and disabled, the Guardian had sent out the names of more than 14,000 Clark County voters.

By my calculations well over 5,000 emails, predominantly condemnatory of the exercise, had been poured into various Guardian queues by the middle of this week. Emails received by individual journalists accounted to about 3,000 of those.

On Monday G2 carried an unexpurgated selection of the correspondence under the restrained heading (considering the invective): Dear Limey assholes. The selection was thinly sprinkled with letters praising the venture. The aggressively abusive letters prompted more than 90 from Americans apologising for their compatriots.

The majority of emails received up to Thursday, whether from supporters of George Bush or John Kerry, were critical (only about one in 10 voiced support). It was clear that a 'spamming' campaign was involved. One Guardian journalist, with dual American and British nationality – a strong supporter of the exercise – believed the reaction illustrated the intimidatory tactics of the angry right. The response of Democrats, fearing that their cause would be harmed, showed that the intimidation worked. The intention was to smother free speech. The G2 exercise sought to open up debate.

Having read through many of the emails, and while acknowledging the letters of thanks and support among them, my own view is that the paper, in carrying out the exercise through the intrusive use of the voters' list, has prejudiced some of the goodwill it has built up in America and unnecessarily excited its enemies. It has sought to intervene in the US election, with unpredictable consequences.

In a poll I conducted among staff who had been following the story, of 71 respondents, 13 thought it a legitimate and worthwhile exercise, 14 were undecided and 44 were against it. Among the reasons given by the latter, reflecting complaints coming from the US, were that intervention in the democratic processes of another country was not 'legitimate newspaper behaviour'; and that it was arrogant and self-aggrandising.

Several were dismayed that the internet effect had apparently not been anticipated, one saying that the speed with which links to the Guardian story spread showed that 'this perceived insult has legs'. Another commented: 'It seems a shame that, in this interactive age, with email and weblogs all around, we rejected any attempt to have a real conversation with US voters.' Several mentioned that the buoyant and jaunty nature of G2 journalism, marking a cultural distinction from the broadsheet, was not apparent on the website.

The editor of the Guardian, defending the exercise, said it was a crucially important election in the face of which many felt a sense of impotence. 'What we did was simply to invite personal acts of communication from one individual to another. Most of the letters sent by Guardian readers, those I have seen, have been responsible and heartfelt.'

October 23 2004

Comments without context

As I write, an eerie lull has descended on the email queues, recently subjected to two tidal waves of mostly, but not entirely, angry correspondence from the United States.

The first was concerned with the Guardian's one-to-one letter-writing exercise involving the voters of Clark County in Ohio. I have associated myself with those who expressed misgivings about it. This exercise, however, did at least raise issues that will continue to be worth discussing. For instance, what is the difference between the injunction in an editorial urging citizens in the US to vote for John Kerry and the more direct stimulation of personal letters from individual readers of the Guardian to individual voters in a finely balanced area of a marginal or swing state in the US?

Did the exercise have any effect on the outcome? Some people in the US clearly think it did. I have had emails from triumphant or disconsolate citizens, one containing a picture of Kerry supporters looking miserably towards the scoreboard. It came with a message: 'From Ohio – with love!? Next time, mind your own business.'

Another, from 'a frustrated Ohio liberal', read: 'Like so many liberals here in the United States, I'm beginning to wonder when to get out.

'It all came down to Ohio in the end … Your efforts, while positive in spirit, caused irreparable harm. What will you do to reach out to us? Anything?' In fact, Dan Harkins, chair of the Clark County Republican party, told the features editor that the paper's campaign may have contributed to a turnout of 76.7%, the highest in living memory, but he indicated that he thought any effect beyond that was unlikely.

The fact is that we have no way of knowing whether the exercise had any impact on the outcome or not. What would we be saying had Clark County gone to Mr Kerry against a national tendency?

The second wave of emails was concerned with comments in a Saturday column of television criticism in which the writer, having forlornly predicted a victory for George Bush, invoked the names of several notorious assassins. I was in the foothills of the Dolomites the following day when a telephone call alerted me to this. The article had already been removed from the website. On Monday, the first publication day of the Guardian after the appearance of the offending article, a total retraction and apology was published.

I have sampled the emails in this second wave and if anything they reached an even higher pitch of outrage. No one can be surprised by this. The comments were indefensible. I said as much to a caller from Boston, Massachusetts, earlier this week.

She was pleased, up to a point, to hear about the Guardian's response. 'But,' she said, 'those comments are now out there and that is something that I find scary.'

I want to take up her point, without in any way diminishing the condemnation of the remarks of which she and so many others complained. Both of these controversies stemmed from material published not in the main broadsheet, news and comment section but in supplements. Clark County was published in G2, the tabloid second section of the Guardian. The reference to various assassins was published in a column (often vituperative) that appeared on page 52 of the small-format (A5) entertainments guide published every Saturday.

Both of these publications have their own characters, distinct from each other and from the broadsheet paper. I mentioned the particular character of G2 in my earlier column. The Guide, host to the piece which caused the second wave, has achieved and maintains credibility with the (mainly) young audience addicted to it by sharing language and, usually, attitudes.

These distinctions begin to disappear when the material is put up on the website. They disappear almost entirely when linked from the home page. And there is no context whatsoever when they are picked up by bloggers.

Blogs, particularly, in the United States, played a big part in the dissemination of the comments in the second case. They do not usually want to give or even hint at context. They are often slow to pick up retractions or apologies. This 'web effect' is something to which the Guardian, and other multi-section newspapers, need to give more thought. Is it possible to avoid providing gifts to political opponents without emasculating the content of the paper?

November 6 2004

Click here for free speech

Should the Guardian provide links from its website to material on other websites that it would not itself publish? This was a question we had to consider in relation to the Nuremberg Files, the website put up by anti-abortionists in the US, the American Coalition of Life Advocates, naming more than 200 doctors who had performed or were prepared to perform abortions.

The site listed not only names but also addresses, car registration numbers and family details. Murdered doctors, such as Dr Barnett Slepian, who was shot by a sniper, remained on the website but with a line scored through their names. The National Abortion Federation in the US argued that the site and the motivation for it should be considered against a violent background which included the death of three doctors, 16 attempted murders, 39 bombings and 99 acid attacks.

Last week a court in Oregon awarded damages of more than £60m to doctors who successfully argued that their safety had been threatened by the publication of this list. Those responsible for the site were found to be in breach of a fairly recent law banning the use of force or the threat of force against people seeking or providing legal abortions.

All this was reported in the Guardian. The only illustration carried in the main paper, on our front page on February 4, was a graphic from the Nuremberg Files website carrying the words: 'Visualise Abortionists On Trial ... New: Horrible Pictures Smuggled From Baby-Butcher Lab!' There appeared to be agreement among senior journalists that we would not have published more than that, and definitely not pictures of the website page showing the names.

On the day of the court's decision we said in a leader: 'The internet did not create the challenge of balancing free speech against the right to privacy, but it has intensified the problems.'

And later: 'Free speech is not absolute and has to be placed in context.' So to return to the question. In our own website coverage of the matter, should we have provided a link to the Nuremberg Files site, a site which did contain material that we would not ourselves have published? My own initial feeling was that we should not. Others thought we should, and, in fact, we did. We maintained a link with the site until a few days ago, when it was dismantled. Who was right? The editor of the website argued that for anyone using the internet it would be an extremely simple matter to find the Nuremberg site. He felt that in making it possible at the click of a mouse to look at the site at the centre of the controversy the Guardian was indicating its trust in the maturity of readers to make up their own minds.

No one, neither he nor I, had the confidence that he was absolutely right. During the Pinochet extradition row, we provided a link to General Pinochet's own site, even though many consider him to be a mass murderer. No one thought there was anything wrong with that. But clearly there are occasions when we would not provide links. We would not, if we were running a story about child pornography on the net, provide a link to a site containing it (to argue that it would not be quite that simple, or actually illegal, dodges the issue). If we were reporting on a site carrying instructions for the manufacture of a bomb, we would not link to that.

So clearly there is a point, disregarding legal constraints, beyond which our instinct towards free speech would not carry us. The editor of the Guardian, like the website editor, is strongly in favour of providing links, unless there is a clear reason not to do so. He feels it is a service to the reader. He points out that the internet is the most democratic medium ever invented. We are, he suggests, in a period like the end of the 18th century, characterised by great struggles over freedom of speech. He believes there are limits ('free speech is not absolute', as we said in our leader) but that the decision to click on to the Nuremberg Files site was on the right side of the boundary.

There is one point which may seem to argue against my own view. That is that anyone visiting the Nuremberg Files site through the Guardian's website would have been doing so within the context of our own reporting of the affair. This, because of the nature of the internet, and the ease with which it can provide links to related material, has been much broader, almost infinitely broader one is tempted to say, than we would have been able to provide in the paper. As for the Nuremberg link: what would you have done?

February 13 1999

The deletion of a report on the website

On Wednesday, journalists on the Guardian's website were alerted to a story running in the German press, in which the US deputy defence secretary, Paul Wolfowitz, was said to have admitted, in effect, that oil was the main reason for the war in Iraq. The German sources were found, translated, and at 4.30pm that day a story sourced to them was posted on the website under the heading 'Wolfowitz: Iraq war was about oil'.

Mr Wolfowitz, in fact, had said nothing of the kind, as a deluge of email, most of it from the US, was quick to point out. Some of it registered disappointment more than anything else – disappointment that a valued source of news and liberal comment had in this instance let them down. 'The briefest of searches will bring up articles to totally discredit your story,' one complained.

Many correspondents seized the opportunity the paper had provided to attack it. One wrote from Chicago: 'Thousands of people all over the world read your paper's internet edition. It is a global journalistic presence and a global force ... In the past year I have seen your paper abandon any pretext of objectivity and become little more than agitprop for the Bush-haters' club.' Another called the report 'part of what appears to be ... an ongoing media campaign to discredit Jews in general and Mr Bush in particular'.

Here is one in the disappointed category: 'You make it sound [as though Mr Wolfowitz] was saying the US had to go to war for economic reasons because it needed the Iraqi oil, when what he was really saying was that ... economic sanctions and incentives didn't work with Iraq because of the oil revenue. I'm no fan of the Bush administration – but this is blatant manipulation. If you want to condemn the Bushies there are sufficient facts ... without inventing them. My trust in the integrity of your newspaper rests upon a prominent retraction in tomorrow's edition.'

By 4.30pm on Thursday, about 24 hours after it was posted, the report was deleted. A statement to that effect was posted prominently on the home page of the website. It was amended at about 5.30pm to take in more of the precise words of Mr Wolfowitz, which were available on the website of the US defence department.

That statement remained on the home page of the website until about 6.30pm. At that time all the corrections that were published on the leader page of Friday's print edition, with the Wolfowitz correction leading, were made available to the website, several hours earlier than usual.

Unusual efforts were made not only to correct but to kill the story because it was wrong and by Thursday morning was attracting worldwide interest. There were telephone calls from media organisations in South Africa and New Zealand, for example, seeking to check it. It provided another example of the speed with which information (and misinformation), spreads through the internet. The paper has done its best to send a frank correction in pursuit and I repeat it here: 'A report which was posted on our website on June 4 under the heading "Wolfowitz: Iraq war was about oil" misconstrued remarks made by the US deputy defence secretary, Paul Wolfowitz, making it appear that he had said that oil was the main reason for going to war in Iraq. He did not say that. He said, according to the department of defence website, "The ... difference between North Korea and Iraq is that we had virtually no economic options with Iraq because the country floats on a sea of oil. In the case of North Korea, the country is teetering on the edge of economic collapse and that I believe is a major point of leverage whereas the military picture with North Korea is very different from that with Iraq." The sense was clearly that the US had no economic options by means of which to achieve its objectives, not that the economic value of the oil motivated the war. The report appeared only on the website and has now been removed.'

That has not satisfied all the paper's critics. There is no total satisfaction in these situations. The story should not have run. In view of the significance of the statements attributed to Mr Wolfowitz, rigorous checking should have taken place. The hazard of translating remarks from German back into the English in which they were originally made should have been apparent.

June 7 2003

Chasing a mistake with the truth

Two weeks ago this column reported the deletion from the Guardian's website of a story that falsely said the US deputy defence secretary, Paul Wolfowitz, had stated that oil was the main reason for the war in Iraq. The report was on the site for less than 24 hours, but during that brief span it was picked up and circulated by readers and news media all over the world. Extraordinary efforts were made to kill it. A lengthy correction, reporting Mr Wolfowitz's words from a transcript on the department of defence website, was carried on Guardian Unlimited, initially and unprecedentedly on the homepage. The same retraction led the corrections column of the printed paper the following morning. It was repeated in my Saturday column.

After the publication of the correction on both the website and in the paper, a letter was dispatched to the Guardian from Mr Wolfowitz's office, protesting at the error and quoting, as the retraction had done, Mr Wolfowitz's actual words at the Asia security conference in Singapore on May 31. The letter also pointed out remarks that Mr Wolfowitz made on June 3, at a press conference at the US embassy in Tokyo, in which he said, in part: 'The notion that the war was ever about oil is a complete piece of nonsense.' In addition, it referred to remarks he made in Washington on February 27, in which he said, again in part: 'If we have to go to war – and I still hope we don't have to go to war – this will not be a war for oil.' The letter, from Mr Wolfowitz's special adviser, Kevin Kellems, concluded with what the Guardian had, in effect, already conceded: 'It is beyond debate that the deputy secretary's view on this important topic was grossly mischaracterised in the Guardian.'

The correction and the column clearly reached a great many of those who received the original and wrong story. For example, the Namibian, in Windhoek, which had picked up the false story, on the following Monday carried a shortened version of the retraction. About 300 emails responding to the publication of the correction and to my column arrived over the next few days. They came from, among other places, Australia, Taiwan, Thailand, Jordan, Finland, Germany, the Netherlands, Mexico and Canada, but predominantly from the US. Among the relatively few from Britain was one from Gregory Djerejian, an American in London, who runs a weblog, Belgravia Dispatch, which was one of the first to jump on the error. He pointed out that in Pravda the story had been 'distorted even more'.

Some correspondents suggested the story was the product of institutional anti-Americanism, something strongly rejected by the editor of the Guardian and by the editor-in-chief of Guardian Unlimited. Several million people in the US look at the Guardian site each month. Most of them, the editor of the paper says, do not confuse criticism of the Bush administration with hostility towards the US or the American people. However, they rightly demand accuracy.

The editor-in-chief of Guardian Unlimited, who has been examining the checks and referrals in her department, says: 'We are a left-of-centre publication. That may influence the stories we are interested in, but it does not absolve us from telling the truth. That is why we deleted this story and carried a correction.'

A majority of readers from left and right commended the speedy retraction. A reader from Ohio wrote: 'I am a Bush supporter ... and as such am not a big fan of the Guardian ... I think your coverage of the Bush administration and Iraq war ... has been horribly biased and distorted. That being said, I appreciate your prompt response to criticism and your lengthy explanation of the reasons for the retraction ... I found it refreshing that you responded in the fashion that you did.'

There was a similar response from a 'rightwing, pro-Bush, pro Iraq-liberation American' in Pennsylvania, who said: 'I am satisfied with your apology ... I read the Guardian because some of your reporting is top notch and a useful oppositional check on my own decidedly biased world view.' Another Bush supporter wrote: 'Even though I disagree with your editorial slant, your quick and detailed retraction shows an integrity that is often lacking in the press.'

I was unable to restrain a rare smile at this comment from a reader in California: 'I find it amusing that only the liberal papers are "correcting" themselves (but only when called out on their mistakes). You seldom find "conservative" papers having to do the same.'

June 21 2003

When a correction is not enough

A question that often occurs to me, doing what I do, is: how flawed does a report have to be before its overall value is negated? In the case of the error to which I devoted this column a couple of weeks ago, the first question would be: was the overall coverage of the Holocaust commemoration undermined by referring to the concentration camps established by the Nazis in German-occupied Poland as 'Polish death camps'?

The answer to that particular question is, no, of course not. It was one serious mistake in one piece (albeit a leader). The answer is no also because of the speed with which the error was acknowledged and corrected, and followed swiftly by the lengthier discussion and apology from the editor, which was contained in my column. Indeed, applying the same question only to the specific leader in which the mistake occurred, the answer might still be no, because the sentiments the column was expressing were clear and considered praiseworthy even by some of those objecting, rightly, to that particular phrase.

The objections of those who complained contained, among other elements, two important and understandable points. One was that the description was in any case wrong. That was true whether or not the question was considered in the context, mentioned by some later correspondents, of anti-semitism in Poland at the time. And the other point was that the phrase, if allowed to stand uncorrected as time removed us further from the period, might more readily be taken literally by those ignorant of the history.

This last point was possibly the primary reason why the Guardian, among a number of other news organisations in the United Kingdom and elsewhere, was the target of a determined lobby, one that on this occasion was indeed pushing at an open door.

Journalists still sometimes express the fear – not very often at the Guardian now – that following a course that involves a quick and public acknowledgment of serious error somehow detracts from their status and credibility, and from the credibility of the paper, whereas I believe it often, and perhaps usually, has the opposite effect.

It is the anger and conflict that build up in the absence of acknowledgment that more commonly do the damage. It is worth considering the clash between the BBC and the government over the Andrew Gilligan broadcast (in which the BBC reporter suggested that Downing Street knew that the government's Iraq weapons dossier contained a claim that it knew to be false) in that context.

It is well to be aware of or to try to discern the motivation of lobbies. They are sometimes concerned quite simply with getting a particular point corrected, but not very often in my experience. Sometimes the motivation is readily understandable and acceptable, as in the case of the concerted attempt to banish the phrase 'Polish death camps'. In that case we in effect join the lobby. (Incidentally, that offending phrase persists, despite corrections by the Guardian and Channel 4 News, occurring since then, for example, in the London Evening Standard.)

Sometimes it seems reasonable to suppose the motivation is not simply the pursuit of a correction and that the intention is to discredit the particular report or commentary by holding up the flaw as an example of an overall failure or unreliability. What the coordinator of this kind of lobby does in such a case is to place on its own website a report that asks or implies the question, 'If they got this wrong, what else did they get wrong?' Or, 'They've been forced to admit that they got this wrong, so perhaps you'll believe us when we say they got the rest of it wrong.' Forced is a favourite word, not so much of individuals but of members of lobbies (which is not quite the same thing) who have sought and obtained a correction that in most cases required no forcing at all.

It is not going too far to say that some lobbies seek to go beyond the point of discrediting a particular report, attempting instead to discredit a particular journalist or going even further to discredit the messenger, in this case the Guardian, particularly in its role as a global publisher through its website. They will do this because of the degree of trust it commands as a source of (usually) reliable news. One of the purposes, perhaps the main purpose, of correcting things the paper gets wrong, with or without lobby pressures, is to maintain that trust. Paradoxically that makes the Guardian a target for lobbies.

To return to the opening question. We have discussed in this column before reports that are not just wrong, but totally wrong. They are, however, rarer than some lobbies suggest.

February 19 2005

A report restored

On April 14 this year, the Guardian published a comment page article by freelance investigative writer Duncan Campbell headlined, 'The ricin ring that never was'. The subheading read: 'Yesterday's trial collapse has exposed the deception behind attempts to link al-Qaida to a "poison attack" on London'.

Mr Campbell, who is not to be confused with the staff journalist of the same name, had been asked to give evidence in his capacity as a scientific expert witness on computers and telecommunications. He had been able to show that a small number of documents, which it was claimed could only have been obtained as a result of terrorist training in Afghanistan, could in fact have been downloaded at any internet cafe in the United Kingdom.

I do not intend to go into details of the case. However, in the course of his piece, Mr Campbell had named two scientific witnesses from the military research establishment at Porton Down whose identity, the Ministry of Defence quickly pointed out, had been protected by the court. The ministry, in a letter to Mr Campbell and the Guardian, warned that the disclosure of the identity of any Porton Down witness who had been granted anonymity was likely to be in contempt of court. The letter specifically warned against any further disclosure. It has been Mr Campbell's contention throughout that he was unaware that any such order had been made.

In the light of the letter from the Ministry of Defence, the Guardian immediately removed the article from its website. It did so on the advice of its lawyers, who then set out to clarify the situation and in particular to obtain a copy of the relevant order. This was said to be in the form of a public-interest immunity certificate (a PII) which had been submitted to the court on behalf of the defence secretary and had received the approval of the judge. The letter from the legal department of the MoD indicated that the grounds for the application were the need to protect the safety of the witnesses from, it said, 'persons unconnected with the case'.

Despite several requests, the MoD and the Crown Prosecution Service failed to provide a copy of the order. However, its lawyers spoke to the prosecution and defence lawyers in the case, who confirmed that the judge had granted an unopposed application to protect the identity of Porton Down witnesses. Apparently, they were not named in open court and they were screened from the jury when they gave evidence. No order was posted in the court press room – the usual practice with reporting restrictions – and Mr Campbell was not at court.

The article has now been put back on the website with the anonymity of the Porton Down scientists protected. Mr Campbell said: 'The story is in no way damaged by the removal of the names.' The restored version has at the top of it the following note: 'Corrected version: this article has been restored to the website after being removed and corrected following a legal complaint.'

In the interval – roughly six months – between the removal of the article from the website and its restoration a few days ago, a number of conspiracy theories have developed. In particular, the Guardian has been accused of caving in to government pressure exerted through D-notices. In fact, D-notices have not existed since 1993. In that year they became DA notices (defence advisory notices). There are only five of them. They are all to be found on the website www.dnotice.org.uk. They are advisory and the committee responsible for the system has no power of enforcement. It had no involvement of any kind in Duncan Campbell's ricin article.

The Guardian generally goes to great length to keep material in circulation. The questions that remain for the paper include: does it explain quickly enough why something is being taken down, does it get articles back on to the website as soon as it can and does it then tell readers why the article has suddenly reappeared? It has done, for the first time, in the case of the ricin report.

October 24 2005

Hands off the archive

Among the advantages of electronic news archives are the speed
and ease with which they can be consulted. A trip to the hernia
land of the bound-newspaper shelves at the public library is now
rarely required and usually only for historical research. To dip
into the more immediate past we need not stir from the keyboard
– and there it all is, no matter how grim or embarrassing, at our
fingertips.

This instant and universal access undoubtedly, and rightly,
stimulates the demand for quick corrections. It has also led to an
increasing number of demands for what often seem to me to be
little more than cosmetic touches. These are resisted.

What, a journalist asked me recently, should she do about a
request from someone who, while conceding that he had been
quoted accurately in a report, wanted one particular descriptive
phrase that he had used changed for another? His boss
apparently had made a critical comment that prompted the
request.

The answer to the journalist's question was: do absolutely
nothing. If the change requested would not qualify for a note in
the corrections column – the criteria for which are fairly
generous or rigorous depending on your point of view – then the
archive should not be touched. The fact that the archive is
present and live in a way that it never was before the dawn of the
electronic age raises for some the possibility that history might
very easily be amended to their advantage.

Ideally there should be no invisible mending of the archive.
Reporters and editors now routinely get requests to make some
change to the online version of their stories. They have no
authority to carry out such changes. Requests should either be
passed to the legal affairs department, or, if there are no apparent
legal implications, to my department. The archive is controlled in

this way so that readers who consult a particular report can be confident that it faithfully reproduces the version that appeared in the printed paper, if that is where it originated, or it is clearly marked as a corrected version.

The electronic archives are like interlocking rings. The one to which readers have free access is the Guardian Unlimited archive (the website archive) which is complete from 1998, with some material earlier than that. It incorporates the roughly 12,000 corrections that have been made to Guardian reports in that time. Corrections are added to the top of the reports to which they apply, so they are instantly visible.

The resource most commonly used by Guardian journalists – and not available to readers – is the paper's electronic text archive, now shared with the archives of all the other national daily and Sunday newspapers, except the Financial Times. The Guardian's text archive, containing material dating from 1984, is the oldest of them all. It has been a complete archive since the late 1980s (the Observer's archive began in 1993).

Corrections are made to this once a week, with higher priority given to requests for changes or deletions from the Guardian's lawyers. Corrections, particularly the legal ones, are regularly exchanged between all the participants in this archive. The volume of this traffic would, I think, surprise the readers of the majority of papers that do not have corrections columns.

Beyond this, the Guardian subscribes to the huge LexisNexis commercial archive, for which it pays an annual sum well into six figures. This provides access to 15,000 English-language newspapers, magazines and news wires worldwide, and contains much more. It is used by the Guardian's research department and is also directly available to a limited number of journalists.

A few days ago I saw an impressive demonstration of LexisNexis's CopyGuard system for identifying plagiarism and copyright infringement. It scours the vast field for significant matches which are then highlighted. It looked at a case that I dealt with some time ago, when I found in favour of a magazine that claimed it had been plagiarised. It showed that indeed that had been the case, but it also demonstrated that in the same piece the offending writer had plagiarised another magazine to an even greater extent. Plagiarists beware!

A final word on the archives: a great deal of effort is spent trying to keep them clean and reliable. We try to resist unnecessary tampering. Try not to ask.

February 27 2006

The unlimited life of a redundant review

Almost three years ago the Guardian's food editor visited the Bull & Butcher, a public house and restaurant at Turville in the Chilterns. Both the place and the pub have featured in several popular television series, including The Vicar of Dibley and Midsomer Murders.

The food editor's review appeared in the paper and on the website, where it remains, beneath a heading saying he had found 'a few rich pickings among the offerings at a village pub in the Chilterns'. The heading, I think, fairly describes what follows – a review that praises some things but not others. It comes up in an electronic search, clearly dated at the top of the piece: March 10 2001.

Since that date, however, the pub has changed management. The new landlord recently sent an email to say he had taken over in August 2003. He complained that the review, which appeared on a Google search for Bull & Butcher, in effect, worked against the efforts he and his wife had made to improve things. He said: 'It cannot be good for my pub when people see this.'

He did not ask directly for the review to be removed from the website. He simply inquired about 'the options'. The course he suggested was another visit from the paper to assess the pub as it is now. On the telephone, he made it clear that he was not complaining about the review as such. It was, he said, 'most probably fair'. However, it was outdated and the disparaging parts of it no longer applied. Potential customers were likely to see the review on an internet search, for two principal reasons. One was the fame of the village, exciting a desire to visit it and have a drink or a meal there. The other was that the Bull & Butcher had its own website and an increasing number of customers used it to make reservations online.

What did the food editor actually say in his review? He praised, among other things, the 'real fires, real stone flagstones, real beams, real beer and real food'. He made favourable comments about the size of the portions and, in particular, about the liver that he ordered, saying that whoever cooked it knew exactly what they were about. 'It was impeccable: tender velvet with a crisp veneer.'

He was accompanied on his visit by his mother, his Aged Parent, as he put it. Her meal, in the opinion of both of them, was only good in parts. His conclusion was that in the growing company of gastropubs 'on this showing' – and I emphasise that point – the Bull & Butcher had little to distinguish it from others, 'characterful certainly, but lacking real class'.

Considering the matter now, the food editor has some sympathy with the new landlord. The editor-in-chief of Guardian Unlimited also said she sympathised with him, but the article was clearly dated and formed part of the archive. She was concerned that a precedent would be set that might open the way to frequent amendment or deletion of archived material. The integrity of the archive was at stake.

Normally material is only removed from the archive on the advice of the legal department, or at my request. It is almost always for legal reasons. Offhand, I can recall only one occasion in the past six years when I have asked for something to be deleted – an erroneous report concerning the US deputy secretary of defence, Paul Wolfowitz. So unusual was this that I wrote two articles explaining why, in my view, it had been necessary to do that.

In the present matter, I sought the opinion of one of the Guardian's lawyers. She immediately made the point that anything on the internet is seen as a fresh publication each time it is accessed. The food editor's review if challenged would rely on a defence of fair comment, in other words that, at the time, it reflected honestly held opinion based on accurate facts. That would continue to apply even if the following day, the restaurant had, say, employed a new chef or changed its menu or just had a better day.

It would be unreasonable, she felt, to expect the paper to correct every review to reflect changes since the specific event to which it applied – in this case a clearly dated meal taken in 2001.

In fact, a search brought up another mention on the website, this time from the Observer of July 13, last year, just before the changeover, warmly recommending the Bull & Butcher for its summer barbecues on the lawn.

Future searches should bring up this column, too, telling everyone, clearly enough, I hope, what they surely might assume: that a three-year-old review is no longer guaranteed to apply.

January 31 2004

10.

TRUTH IN PICTURES

There are almost as many things that you can do wrong with a picture as there are with a piece of printed text. I have written more columns about the Guardian's use of pictures, considering them for a moment as a single subject, than about anything else. The column itself, however, has never been illustrated and I have been quite happy about that for most of the time. It might have been useful to have shown how the Guardian manipulated the picture of the bombing of Atocha station in Madrid and to have compared that with the way in which other papers used the same picture. Essentially what I was discussing, though, in the light of a reader's complaint, was the principle of the integrity of the image, a theme that runs through this section.

Manipulation in the sense of altering content by addition or subtraction of images – even by taking out the top of someone's head intruding above the chancellor's red dispatch box on budget day – is forbidden. So, at the Guardian, is the flipping or reversal of images. The flexibility, let us call it, of digital photography and editing in combination with unlimited access to images on the internet creates endless possibilities for hoaxing. The example here of the elk in Thomas Hardy country raises additional questions about citizen journalism. The guiding principle in all this is that readers should be able to believe that the images they see in the Guardian are authentic and unmanipulated – that seeing is believing.

Two pictures that did not tell the right story

I have dealt with two complaints in the past few weeks prompted by photographs which were to an extent misused, with distressing or embarrassing consequences. Both reflect the pressure to illustrate that the highly pictorial nature of the modern Guardian, both in print and online, exerts upon editors working to deadlines.

One complaint involved a photograph of a man in hospital who, despite the fact that his face was partially concealed by his hand, was recognised by his son – or I should say that his son, and the rest of his family, felt that they recognised him beyond any reasonable doubt. Their distress was exacerbated by the fact that their relative had died last year. Further, the photograph was used, on the home page of Guardian Unlimited, to illustrate a report about assisted dying. This was in no way relevant to the death of the complainant's father.

The degree of uncertainty that remained about the identity of the man in the picture did not in the circumstances seem to me to be particularly important. The photograph was taken by a staff photographer in a London hospital in 2001. The Guardian itself now had no way of identifying the man in the picture. At the time, the picture would have been taken with the approval of the hospital and with the consent of the patient who had, presumably, chosen partially to conceal his face. There is absolutely no reason to suppose that any other than the correct procedures were followed.

What was wrong was to use such a picture after it had lain in the archive for five years. The journalists who took the decision believed that the identity of the patient was concealed. The question to ask was perhaps: were this my father, would I recognise him? They perhaps felt they would not. I felt I would.

There are always two other important things to consider with this type of archive picture: one is the possibility that the patient has died since the picture was taken; the other is whether the purpose for which the picture is being reused is appropriate.

The picture has now been deleted from the archive. The Guardian has written to the complainant's mother, the widow of the man the family felt they had identified in the picture, apologising for the distress she and they had felt. Guardian Unlimited is left with questions to ask about picture editing online – I am told that developments are imminent. The picture desk, and for that matter the paper at large, is left with questions about illustrating stories from stock and out of the context in which the pictures were originally taken.

The second complaint came from an England football supporter who was pictured by an agency photographer while in Germany for the World Cup. He was shown in profile wearing a white German army-style helmet bearing the words 'Come On England!', and with the England flag reflected in the lens of his sunglasses (an effect which he was posed to achieve). The picture was taken quite independently and with no knowledge of the way in which it would be used, or by whom it would be used.

In fact, the Guardian used it on its front page in a manner and in a context which I felt provided justifiable cause for complaint. The following note and apology appeared in the corrections column on Saturday: 'We carried above a report headed "Quit the Nazi thing, says our man in Berlin", front page, June 29, about bad-mannered, uncouth English football fans, a picture of a man in a joke German army helmet. We wrongly described this in a caption as "Nazi-style headgear", a phrase that was not used in the caption provided by the photographer who took the picture or his agency. We apologise for any embarrassment caused if this gave the impression that the man in the picture was one of those referred to in the accompanying report. We point out that the hat carried a slogan no more offensive than the words "Come On England!"'

As Harold Evans is supposed to have said: 'The camera cannot lie. But it can be an accessory to untruth.' The correction is now attached to the online version.

July 10 2006

Those flipping photos

During the England-Argentina game in the World Cup we were looking at agency pictures in the Guardian offices in Farringdon Road, London within 15 minutes of their being shot in the stadium in France, thanks to digital technology.

The speed with which high-definition pictures can now be transmitted is one of the more obvious benefits of the technological revolution that has swept over newspaper picture desks. But it has not changed the fact that behind each camera, no matter how advanced the technology, there is a human being, a craftsman or a sullen artist. And it has not diminished the degree of responsibility that journalists have to exercise in handling pictures. The technology has made deception a great deal easier and therefore perhaps more tempting. It means we have to have a clearer idea than ever of what it is right and not right to do. If we move the ball in a football picture to provide a more convenient crop (which newspapers commonly used to do), we are in a sense moving the goalposts, too.

What we consider it legitimate to do is to use the technology now available to carry out the equivalent of normal dark room functions: to crop, lighten, darken, sharpen and very little else, to enhance the image – not to bring sunshine to a rainy day in Birmingham.

Suspicions of tampering are a threat to integrity. At the time of Gordon Brown's first budget, we took out an intrusive clump of hair belonging to someone otherwise obscured by the raised dispatch box. What was simply tidying up to one was a gross deception to another. We took the point and will never do that again. This particular lapse now haunts us as a frequently quoted example of bad practice.

We have – don't I know it – extremely vigilant readers who scrutinise everything we do. They are particularly scathing when they catch us flipping. If we are prepared to flip, to reverse, a picture, either by design or accident, what else might we not be getting up to? The picture editor believes some journalists identify him as the person who looks over their shoulders and mutters 'No flipping!' He could not be more against it.

Nevertheless, we do it quite frequently. Most commonly, when it is done deliberately, it is to serve what is taken (often wrongly) by some as a design tenet: that a person in a picture shall not gaze out of the page but invariably into it. Recently a reader noticed that a head in the teasers above the masthead on page 1 looked one way, while on the page to which he was directed the same head looked in the opposite direction. He did not find this a confidence-inspiring phenomenon.

We quite often turn right-handed musicians into left-handers. Not long ago we created an entire left-handed orchestra. However, the title 'flipper of the year', perhaps it should be 'flipper of the millennium', goes to the person who, god-like, flipped our page 1 picture of the Horsehead nebula, providing Guardian readers with a view which, without our assistance, they would have needed to travel for 1,500 light years to obtain. Most of these are accidents produced by pressure rather than deliberate intent, or even incompetence.

The ease with which pictures can be manipulated has increased the anxiety the picture editor has to bear. He relies on the integrity of his sources. When a difficult decision has to be taken over whether a controversial picture should or should not be used, he needs to have complete faith in its authenticity. If it has come from an agency, then his relationship with the agency has to be such that he is confident that his colleagues there have asked all the questions that should be asked.

One example where this confidence was crucial was in our decision to use on the front page the picture of a young woman who had hanged herself from a tree in Bosnia. We were helped on this occasion by the presence there of our own reporter who had borne the burden of witnessing this among many other dreadful events. Its authenticity was still doubted by some, who pointed to all sorts of things in the picture that they took as evidence that it had been fabricated. The picture editor, knowing how easily pictures can now be forged, had to weigh these factors in deciding what to do. We used it big on page 1, and quite rightly, too. It had what very few pictures have: a symbolic weight that said something about the folly and sorrow of war. We have to keep trying to work out what it is, in an age of image bombardment, that gives certain pictures this quality. In an average week, how many Guardian pictures would you say are memorable?

July 11 1998

The cautionary tale of a citizen hoaxer

On Monday last week the Guardian published a report – accompanied by a dramatic photograph – of a heath fire in Dorset. The report began: 'Canford Heath has blazed before, but rarely like this.' In fact it has never blazed like that. The photograph showed not the fire in Dorset but a forest fire almost six years ago in Montana, the north-western US state bordering Canada.

How did it get into the paper? Seeking to illustrate the story late on Sunday, with no still pictures from the fire in Dorset then available, the picture desk 'grabbed' a selection of images from the rolling news coverage on Sky News. The presenter said on air, while this particular image was held on the screen: 'We have actually got some pretty dramatic pictures our viewers have sent in.'

The report, addressing the picture, said: 'Wild animals, silhouetted by the bright orange inferno in a photograph taken by a local resident, were left to fend for themselves.' The wild animals in fact are elk, which, as one of my correspondents later that day put it, are rarely seen in Dorset.

I can sympathise both with Sky and with the Guardian picture desk for running this picture in, so to speak, the heat of the moment. As the Guardian story made clear, the Dorset fire was a big one, residents in the area had to be evacuated to safety, and it took 170 firefighters from Dorset and neighbouring Hampshire to bring the fire under control.

Sky showed the picture twice on Sunday evening. A spokesperson told me: 'It was one of several sent in by viewers. Once we had established it was a hoax, we pulled it immediately. We do all we can to ensure that email images sent in by viewers are genuine, but it's inevitable that in a fast-breaking news environment such photos occasionally slip past the checks and balances we put in place.'

The discovery was too late to save us from also falling victim to the hoax. Here is a letter from a reader at the University of Essex: 'I was surprised to see [this story] accompanied by a photograph of what appear to be two elk contemplating a forest blaze from the safety of a river. Not only is it remarkable that wild elk and evergreen forests are flourishing in Dorset, but I was impressed by the striking similarity between the Guardian photograph and one illustrating the front cover of a book which I happen to be using for my PhD research.'

Indeed, there it is, on the cover of Cass R Sunstein's Laws of Fear (Cambridge University Press, 2005), easily found on Amazon. It provides a caption which gives the picture a title, Elk Bath, and says that it was taken on August 6 2000, on the east fork of the Bitterroot River, Montana. The photographer was John McColgan, a fire behaviour analyst from the Alaska Fire Service.

Several other readers directed me to www.snopes.com, a website run by Barbara and David P Mikkelson, specialising in 'urban legends' and performing a very useful service separating fact from fiction. They provide a lot more information. McColgan took the picture with a digital camera and downloaded it on to his office computer, where a friend found it and emailed it to another friend ... It spread on the internet, well, like a forest fire, but rarely carrying authentic caption details. Snopes.com points out that it has been said to show a fire in Yellowstone National Park in 1988 and a forest fire in British Columbia in 2003, among other attributions - all a long way from the land of Thomas Hardy.

I tell all this as a cautionary tale of our time. The picture editor said it points up a problem with 'citizen' journalism. Picture agencies, such as AP and Reuters – the Guardian, too – he reminds us, have draconian rules about altering pictures or passing them off as something they are not – photographers have been sacked for that sort of thing. There are no such rules for the citizen and we do not have the reassurance the rules should bring that seeing is believing.

Sky News, the Guardian, and the news media in general, strive for veracity through vigilance. Who can you trust?

March 27 2006

Madrid: the integrity of the image

On Friday March 12 2004 the Guardian carried across the full width of its front page a colour photograph of the scene at Atocha station in Madrid after what the accompanying story described as 'the worst terrorist attack in Europe since the Lockerbie bombing'.

On Tuesday this week the corrections and clarifications column on the leader page of the paper began with the following item: 'The page 1 photograph ... showing the immediate aftermath of the terrorist attack at Atocha station in Madrid was digitally altered to remove colour and reduce the impact of a severed limb in the foreground. We should have indicated that it had been done and preferably explained why it had been done. The paper has a rule that its pictures are not altered.'

The rule in question, included in the Guardian's editorial code, reads: 'Digitally enhanced or altered images, montages and illustrations should be clearly labelled as such.' The code of the Press Complaints Commission cautions against the use of 'misleading or distorted material including pictures', a breach that would perhaps be difficult to argue in this case.

The rule has been applied scrupulously, noting even such aberrations as the accidental flipping of a photograph of the Horsehead nebula.

Here is an email, written on March 12, protesting at the then unacknowledged interference with the picture: 'I travelled back from Spain today with a copy of El País. Their cover photograph of yesterday's atrocity in Madrid was the same one printed in your newspaper ... In the Spanish newspaper a bloody human limb is clearly visible in the left foreground. This has been removed completely from [another British newspaper's] photograph, and has clearly been treated in some way by you.

Why? My feeling is either print the photo or don't. Are we not grown up enough here for the truth?'

A report on the website which looked at the way in which other papers had used the picture – more than one had altered it – caused a reader to complain that the Guardian was being less than forthright about its own actions.

'Only by reading to the end of the piece ... does one discover that the Guardian also "altered" and "cleaned up" the detached limb by greying it out so it resembled a rucksack. What the Guardian did was use a moral loophole – that the arm still existed on the screen but was essentially unrecognisable – as a cover for shielding readers from information it did not want to convey.'

If the paper was confident enough in its reasons for interfering with the image it should have given them at the time. The daily corrections and clarifications column provides a ready place to carry that kind of explanation. The note that appeared there on Tuesday could have appeared there on Friday, the day the picture was published.

The reasons it might have given would be: deference to the families of the dead and injured; protection of its readers from an unnecessarily gory and distressing detail. It might have argued that the alteration of that detail was irrelevant to the impact of what remained an essentially true record of a horrific event.

We were not given the opportunity to be persuaded by or to reject those or any other reasons. Why does it matter? It is essential, if readers are to believe what they see in the paper, that no internal editing of a presented image takes place. If it does, readers should be told about it straight away.

All newspapers faced the same set of options: print the whole picture in colour without alteration; print the whole picture in black and white, thus making the detail at issue unreadable; digitally remove the detail completely; crop the lower part of the picture to remove the detail; use a completely different picture.

All of those options, except the first, were followed last Friday by one British newspaper or another. What would you have done?

Both the editor of the Guardian and the deputy editor (news) told me that the decision was taken with the best of intentions and against a deadline. They now thought, with hindsight, that it had been a mistake to alter the colour.

A final point. Apart from those who objected to the manipulation of the picture, no one at all complained about it. Had the image been shown unaltered, as it was by El País and other European papers, would you have complained? Since all the main British papers acted on the day in some way to soften the impact or totally avoid the issue, we can ask: is there a reality that others are prepared to face and we are not?

March 20 2004

Footsteps in the snow

About a week ago the Guardian published a photograph captioned, 'Spring flowers seem to be surviving the snowstorm, just, in Edinburgh'. It was credited to David Cheskin and the agency that employs him, the Press Association.

A little before 8pm that day the PA put out what it called a 'mandatory kill' – an order, in other words, that the picture was not to be published and was to be wiped from picture archives. Too late of course for the Guardian and a number of other papers.

The notice, transmitted in red with a full colour reproduction of the withdrawn picture, said: 'It has been brought to our attention that areas of the image have been digitally cloned.' The retraction was clear and unequivocal.

The handbook to the editorial code monitored by the Press Complaints Commission says: 'The PCC insists that if a picture is not what it seems, or if it has been posed or digitally manipulated, the reader should generally be told.'

Manipulating pictures that have the trusted purpose of showing us some piece of reality is no small matter, even if all we are talking about, as in this case, is a flowerbed.

On Tuesday (March 1 2005) this note appeared in the corrections column: 'A photograph of spring flowers flourishing in several centimetres of snow in Edinburgh was digitally altered ... The agency, which supplied the picture in good faith, discovered after publication that image cloning had taken place.'

The editor of the PA told me that the photographer had said that he had been 'doodling' with the image on Photoshop, the digital picture editing system, and had then accidentally filed the wrong image. The PA has accepted his explanation.

Nevertheless, the matter was being taken extremely seriously, I was told, and among other measures the editor and picture editor had recirculated the PA's guidelines on the electronic handling of pictures. These start with the statement: 'The integrity and credibility of the content of the PA picture wire is of paramount importance. The content of a photograph must never be changed or manipulated.'

They make it clear that digital processing should be confined to 'cropping; sharpening; correction of overall exposure, contrast or colour balance; the repair of mechanical defects, such as dust, hair on the sensor, or scratches on the original negative; and any local dodging or burning [another way of saying image enhancement] consistent with that which could have been achieved in a traditional "wet" darkroom. This must not be done to the extent that detail is removed from the picture. Adding, moving or removing anything which changes the content of the image is not permitted.'

The Guardian also has a rigid rule that pictures must not be manipulated, which extends to banning the reversing of images for design or any other purpose. In this column in March last year I criticised the paper for breaking its own rule and manipulating a picture taken in the aftermath of the bombing of Atocha station in Madrid. In that, the colour had been removed from a severed limb in the foreground of the picture, rendering it unreadable.

To put the matter in perspective: the picture desk receives about 5,500 digital images a day. Between 120 and 150 images are chosen for publication from those and from other sources. Readers are quick to query pictures that they feel show signs of manipulation. On Monday this week (February 28) we published a picture headed: 'Cold war – North Korean children take aim at America'. It showed children apparently throwing snowballs at a snowman representing the United States. A reader wrote: 'A fairly casual inspection of this rather feeble bit of North Korean propaganda makes it obvious that the snowman was never in the original photo, but merely inserted afterward.'

The editor of the section felt that the statement in the caption that the photograph was 'released by the state Korean Central News Agency' announced clearly enough that it was a piece of propaganda. But he suggests it might have been spelt out more directly.

Whether it was manipulated or not we do not know. The reader thinks it was and I think he is probably right. It was presented as an example of propaganda, and manipulation is its useful tool. It taints the user.

March 5 2005

11.

SENSITIVITY

Most of the issues discussed in this section may appear to be simply matters of taste. However, as is nearly always the case, they go beyond the purely subjective question of our own reaction and imply an attitude to others that appears to place the writer and the views expressed in conflict with the liberal, inclusive values that define the Guardian. One of the principal values is the right to freedom of speech, and the question of the compatibility of free speech with sensitivity to the feelings or condition of others is very often a consideration.

The first column here, written in my first month in the role of readers' editor, looks at the way in which the Weekend magazine treated the subject of pornography and notes in passing that the Guardian has no guidelines on the use of four-letter words. Now it does have such guidelines, and you will be able to question their effectiveness when the subject comes up again in the next section.

There are two articles here about the reporting of suicide, both arguing the need for there to be some cautionary reference to it in the industry code monitored by the Press Complaints Commission. In August 2006, following the case described below, where I express the hope that it might be catalytic in bringing change, the PCC did in fact ratify the following sub-clause: 'When reporting suicide, care should be taken to avoid excessive detail about the method used.' Adherence to a clause that was introduced into the Guardian's own code several years ago with a similar purpose – of minimising the risks of copycat suicides – has not inhibited discussion of the topic in any way.

Among the other columns here is one that looks at the legitimacy of applying humour in an area which, we might agree, requires the utmost sensitivity – in referring to Alzheimer's disease. As on many other occasions, the result of my own inquiries into that somewhat surprised me.

A poor show for hard porn

Last Saturday, our magazine, Guardian Weekend, ran a cover story about hard-core pornography in the United States. It attracted more complaints than any other single item in the paper over the past month.

Two of the 16 letters, several of which were accompanied by torn-out pages from the magazine and notices of cancellation, are published in Guardian Weekend today. One is from a reader who says, 'You have the right to discuss pornography. But I have the right to protect my children from degrading and offensive pictures of women.' The other accuses us, in effect, of sinking into the morass the article set out to describe. It points out that the author 'omitted to interview a single woman' in the course of a piece of more than 5,000 words spread over eight pages.

The principal cause of complaint was the pictures. One of these was a full-page photograph of a group of four people, one of whom, a woman, appeared to be masturbating. On another page, there were juxtaposed photographs of two pornographers, one with his face a couple of inches from the rear of a naked woman, the other embracing a near-naked and apparently very young girl.

These last two photographs appeared opposite a full-page ad for toys (farm animals) for two- to five-year-olds.

There was anguish, more than anger, in many of the letters. 'This is my first complaint after 45 years as a Guardian reader and enthusiast – who on earth can justify printing this selection of photographs?' One woman wrote, 'Sadly the choice for me is not between the Guardian and another paper, but between sticking with the Guardian and taking no daily paper at all.' This was clearly not a gender or generation issue. The strength of feeling about the piece was common to men and women, and readers who spanned a wide age range. Some readers saw the piece as a symptom of lowering standards, also indicated by an increasing use of four-letter words. In this article, the word 'fuck' – which at present occurs far more frequently in the Guardian than any other serious newspaper in the United Kingdom – cropped up half a dozen times, always in quotes and often in the context of explicit description of the pornographer's activities.

One colleague, unconnected with this piece, lamented, 'It's the classic liberal trap. We believe that everything is up for discussion, but any way we do it, we're going to be wrong.' What were we trying to do? The article began with great promise. The writer, quoting US News and World Report, told us that last year Americans spent $8bn on 'hard-core videos, peep shows, live sex acts, adult cable programming, sexual vices, computer porn and sex magazines – an amount much larger than Hollywood's domestic box-office receipts and larger than all the revenues generated by rock and country music recordings'. It referred to unsuccessful attempts to control and contain the growth of the industry. It showed how it was quick to exploit advances in electronic media. It argued that pornography had become a significant element in American culture.

It was on the extended tour of the industry which then followed that difficulties arose. We were introduced to leading pornographers, given a detailed account of their activities and they addressed us in their own language.

The writer of the article says he now recognises it as a weakness that no interviews with women were included. One woman was interviewed but the result was discarded before the writer submitted the piece because her language was so foul.

The editor responsible for last week's magazine said she did not accept that the way in which the porn industry works was described in a sensational way. The pictures were chosen to give some idea of the ethos and tackiness of the industry. It was deemed a subject worthy of interest, partly because of the possible spread of the phenomenon to Britain. The person responsible for the pictures said that great care went into their selection. Those chosen were the mildest available. No one had seen the ad for toys before publication.

A characteristic of the complaints was the genuine dismay of the readers. There was one positive letter responding to points made in the article.

In my opinion, this was a perfectly legitimate subject that demanded a greater awareness and sensitivity than it received. Insufficient thought was given to the effect of the pictures. There is no established practice of looking in advance at the advertisements which will appear on pages carrying sensitive material. The Guardian at present has no readily accessible guidelines on the use of four-letter words. Had guidelines been available, those handling this article might have been alerted to other aspects of it.

The reader who said 'I think you owe an apology to our poor kids' was right.

November 29 1997

Humorous hyperbole or xenophobia?

Beware of the horns of a bull, of the heels of a horse, of the smile of an Englishman.

Irish proverb

Many of you write to me in a state of perplexity at the generalised insults offered now and again through the pages of the Guardian at whole groups or – stimulated recently by the World Cup – entire nations.

On Friday last week one Guardian columnist discussed the proposition that, in the words of the heading, 'Anti-German feeling seems to be the last acceptable prejudice'. It is reasonable to ask whether all his colleagues share his conclusion that 'no prejudice is acceptable'. He went on: 'Open the door to one form of xenophobia and you will soon find yourself well and truly swamped.'

This is the kind of thing my correspondents expect from the Guardian – a call to reason and reasonableness when the mob is roused. However I do not have to dig far into my postbag to find complaints directed at the Guardian for publishing the kind of stereotypical remarks about the Germans that the article was discussing. Exercises of this kind should, perhaps, be viewed with a degree of scepticism.

The bewilderment of some of you is expressed in terms similar to the following, which comes from a reader complaining about what he saw as a recent unfair attack on the Irish in the context of the World Cup: 'Why is [the columnist] allowed to vent his petulant jealousies in a supposedly "liberal" newspaper which just a few days ago was urging us all to get over our "tribalism"?'

This particular column prompted more than 100 complaints. It had the distinction of rousing a previously unknown (to me that is) Irish lobby which accounted for a proportion of the mail.

When I took the complaints to the relevant section editor, he plucked handfuls of hair from his head, complained that the whole thing had been misconstrued and that we were experiencing a (partly) orchestrated humour lapse.

Exactly what did the columnist say that aroused such ire? In the course of a quite short piece, headed 'Cheer the Irish? Never', he registered his dismay at the result of the Ireland-Saudi Arabia game. 'I was cheering for the Saudis, out of a respect for their criminal justice system. Given a choice between two right-of-centre agrarian theocracies, I'll go with the more rigorous one, if that's OK.' By the time the column appeared, Ireland had been knocked out by Spain: 'Who will the world cheer for now that the lovable leprechauns have been returned to their misty hills and treacherous bogs?'

One reader wrote: 'I was surprised that your paper, which I believed to be enlightened, would carry such a piece of hatred. Nice to see that the English tradition of fair play and tolerance lives on. I believe in freedom of speech, but ... Imagine the shoe being on the other foot.'

A reader from Dublin enquired whether the columnist knew the Guardian was widely available in Ireland. 'I myself wander down my own little misty hill and traverse a particularly treacherous bog every morning to get my copy, although in future I'll be binning any supplement containing that patronising git's column.'

That is enough to give a flavour of the more moderate responses. The columnist is dismayed that what he thought was humorous hyperbole or irony aimed at stereotyping should apparently go so wide of the mark. 'Does anyone really think that I believe the Saudi and Irish regimes are similar?'

The features editor defends the column. The target, he says, was not the Irish but the international and implicitly patronising love affair with the Irish football team – the cliched view of the Irish promoted by their part-time international fan club.

Clearly then, this intention passed by a fairly large number of readers. Several of you suggested that similar remarks would not be allowed about, say, black or Jewish people. The editor of the paper believes that considerable care should be taken not to offend people who have recently been or are at present the objects of discrimination.

You may ask whether that goes far enough. I do not think too much should be made of the case I have been discussing. It is a yellow card, not a red one. But does it represent a tendency?

I have pointed out before that the Press Complaints Commission protects individuals and not groups, arguing for reasonable freedom of speech. It throws responsibility back on the individual journalist. Is it in safe hands?

July 1 2002

Inadequate rules on suicide reporting

Two national newspapers, the Times and the Sun, and the London Evening Standard, carried pictures earlier this month of a woman leaping to her death from a Kensington hotel. Another showed her standing on a high ledge before jumping. Like most other papers, the Guardian considered the pictures and rejected any idea of using them – the right decision.

As I write, the Press Complaints Commission (PCC) has before it a number of complaints, including one from Samaritans. Their chief executive was quoted on the Media Guardian website expressing dismay at 'the gratuitously distressing coverage' – an assessment with which I agree.

Samaritans complained that the illustrated coverage breached clause 5 of the editors' code that is monitored by the PCC. That clause in full states: 'In cases involving personal grief or shock, enquiries and approaches must be made with sympathy and discretion and publication handled sensitively. This should not restrict the right to report legal proceedings such as inquests.'

I have argued in the past that this clause does not adequately cover the reporting of suicide and that it totally fails to acknowledge the phenomenon of imitative or copycat suicides. Nowhere in the code, nor in the Editors' Codebook issued by the code committee as a kind of companion to the code, is there any discussion of suicide as an issue requiring special attention.

It thus in effect ignores the advice of frontline organisations such as Samaritans. Samaritans' guidelines for the media state: 'Reports should avoid explicit details of method ... and if possible avoid the use of dramatic photographs or images related to suicide. In retrospective reporting or reconstructions, actual depiction of means should be avoided ...' The purpose of these words is to caution against the dangers of copycat suicides.

As a columnist (Joan Smith), writing in the Independent – which did not report the suicide in words or pictures – put it: 'Suicide … is a special case.'

A good starting point for journalists or for anyone prepared to give this matter serious consideration is the survey conducted a year or two ago by the PressWise Trust charity (now MediaWise: www.mediawise.org.uk). It includes a summary of a survey from the Centre for Suicide Research at the Department of Psychiatry at Oxford University: Suicidal Behaviour and the Mass Media.

MediaWise, in a statement issued immediately after publication of the recent pictures, said: 'The "suicide leap" pictures should not have been published. Evidence from reputable studies conducted over many years indicates the risk of copycat behaviour when this type of coverage occurs.'

MediaWise also reminds us of the wording of a clause it has been advocating as a necessary addition to the editors' code: 'When reporting about suicide or suicide attempts, care should be taken to avoid sensationalism and unnecessary detail, and particular consideration should be given to the likely impact on family … especially children.'

I have advocated something very similar, such as inclusion of the clause that now forms part of the Guardian's own editorial code. This says: 'Guardian journalists should exercise particular care in reporting suicide or issues involving suicide, bearing in mind the risk of encouraging others. This applies to presentation, including the use of pictures, and to describing the method of suicide. Any substances should be referred to in general rather than specific terms. When appropriate a helpline number (eg Samaritans) should be given. The feelings of relatives should be considered.'

It may be that the complaint from Samaritans, since it comes from a third party, will be deemed to fall outside the remit of the PCC. However, the PCC has received, among other complaints, two from close friends of the woman who jumped to her death.

It has launched an investigation into complaints about all three papers concerned. It will be interesting to see if this unfortunate episode will be the catalyst for a significant change in the code.

January 16 2006

A call for a code amendment

The Press Complaints Commission recently revealed that it has 'not upheld' – a nice way of saying rejected – complaints about the publication of pictures in three newspapers of a woman jumping to her death from the fourth floor of a London hotel. It concluded that publication of the pictures, in the Sun, the London Evening Standard and the Times, did not amount to a breach of clause five of the editors' code, which deals with intrusion into grief or shock.

This really comes as no surprise. I have argued – most recently in this column on January 16 this year – that the code as it stands is completely inadequate in relation to suicide. It does not mention it. I said in that column that in the light of everything we now know or should know about suicide, particularly about imitative or copycat suicides, those three newspapers were wrong to publish the pictures, and those papers which chose not to publish them, including the Guardian, were right.

Organisations such as Samaritans have long sought to persuade the media that reporting suicide calls for particular care. What could be more relevant to this case than the following extract from Samaritans' guidelines: 'If possible avoid the use of dramatic photographs or images related to suicide'?

MediaWise, a charitable trust concerned with ethical standards in journalism, has campaigned vigorously, and rightly in my view, for a change in the practice of suicide reporting based upon a knowledge of available research. It has cited, in particular, the study Suicidal Behaviour and the Mass Media, by Kathryn Williams and Keith Hawton of the Centre for Suicide Research at Oxford University. A summary of this and other relevant research has been available for a long time at www.mediawise.org.uk. In addition, MediaWise also offers training programmes for news organisations prepared to accept that this is a matter that warrants special consideration.

MediaWise criticised the publication of these particular pictures as 'irresponsible and reprehensible'. Once again, it drew attention to the research and said: 'The outcry about coverage of [this] tragic death ... should alert editors to the value of having a specific clause in the code of practice and clear in-house policies on responsible coverage.'

The Guardian has a clause in its own editorial code. Here it is in full: 'Suicide: Journalists should exercise particular care in reporting suicide or issues involving suicide, bearing in mind the risk of encouraging others. This applies to presentation, including the use of pictures, and to describing the method of suicide. Any substances should be referred to in general rather than specific terms. When appropriate a helpline number (eg Samaritans, 0845 790 9090) should be given. The feelings of relatives should also be carefully considered.'

I have seen no indication that the Guardian's coverage has been damaged by following this guidance. MediaWise advocates the adoption of a clause which is not dissimilar.

There are at last signs of some movement. The code of practice committee of the Press Complaints Commission – on which the editor of the Guardian serves – has been asked by the commission to consider whether the code 'as it currently stands, is sufficient to cover the reporting of suicide, and any sudden death. This would include whether the code might be amended specifically to address the issue of "copycat" suicides.'

The code committee meets later this week. A couple of weeks ago Press Gazette, a weekly magazine for journalists, made its own editorial comment on the affair. It concluded that it had been wrong for newspapers to carry pictures of the woman in mid-air (choosing to illustrate the point by showing how the Sun had done just that). 'What it does highlight,' it said, 'is the need for the editors' code committee to look more closely at how the code covers reporting suicides. When a flaw is uncovered, it must be put right. That's exactly how self-regulation is supposed to work.'

There is little more to say, is there?

April 24 2006

Journalists and their generation games

One of the ideas I grew up with in journalism, and have never quite grown out of, was that newspapers had the potential to relieve society of its prejudices, or, only slightly more realistically, to ameliorate them. The potential is greater now in the age of the new media than it was when I started 50 years ago. Many of the complaints I deal with are concerned with journalism that does not do that but has the effect of reinforcing prejudice, often by the tedious repetition of stereotypical views.

Let us take age and ageism. In newspapers the latter is perhaps related to an endemic obsession with the former. An obsession with age? A recent report about the death of a witness in the so-called NatWest Three case included an interview with a neighbour of the man and, in quoting her view of him, noted that she was 37. In what scale of values is that a relevant piece of information? In this case it is simply the working of a journalistic reflex.

To come closer to the point, earlier this year the paper started a report of the rescue of two transatlantic sailors with the statement: 'Most retired people are content to fill their days doting on grandchildren, creating their ideal garden, and taking relaxing holidays' – perhaps a pity when the headline was an irreproachable: 'Couple rescued after attempt to sail Atlantic fails'. She was 68; he was 64.

A reader wrote: 'Had the couple been under 25, would the lead have been "Most young people are content to fill their days drinking themselves senseless, watching crap TV, and shagging as much as possible ..."' She suggested an alternative introduction: 'Exemplifying the growing trend for people to take up new challenges in later life ...'

Occasionally the Guardian gets it very wrong, although one of the most recent examples that understandably drew strong complaint from several readers was in the advertising and not the editorial columns. It was a related pair of advertisements. The first showed a grey-haired (and possibly blind) woman at the window of a car, the driver of which had stopped to ask the way. The copy read, 'Want directions you can trust? Turn the page.' Over the page was an advertisement for a satellite navigation system. The Guardian advertising executive who responded to the complainants conceded that they did have a point. The advertisements were not scheduled to appear again.

On the other hand, when in March the cartoonist Steve Bell caricatured the new leader of the Liberal Democrats, Sir Menzies Campbell, as a toothless chicken at a walking frame, no one complained. Sir Menzies Campbell, by the way, is a mere 65.

Sometimes the paper gets it almost startlingly right. Several newspapers carried a story about a 92-year-old woman abseiling down a 220ft tower block. In the Daily Mirror she was Danger Gran. In the Sun she was Action Nan. The Guardian's heading simply said: 'Tower of strength – abseiling at 92 from office block'.

In The Long History of Old Age (Thames and Hudson, 2005), the editor Pat Thane, commenting on the pressures that have brought about changes in the generally acceptable terminology relating to older people, writes: 'Such changes were driven by perceptions of the disparities between a language which constructed people above a certain age as helpless and dependent and the visible reality that increasing numbers of them were not.'

In Ageing Societies (Hodder Arnold, 2006), the director of the Oxford Institute of Ageing, Sarah Harper, writes: 'By 2030 half the population of western Europe will be aged over 50, with a predicted average life expectancy at age 50 of a further 40 years; that is, half western Europe's population will be between 50 and 100 years.' She also notes: 'The group aged 80 years and over is the fastest growing age group in the world' I enter my eighth decade tomorrow. Do you want to make something of it?

July 17 2006

Abuse of a minority already much abused

On January 31 the Guardian's Weekend magazine published the first of two articles by the lesbian feminist Julie Bindel. The column, under the heading 'Gender benders, beware', applauded the decision by the British Columbia supreme court to overturn a ruling that the human rights of Kimberley Nixon, a male-to-female transsexual, had been violated when she was denied the opportunity to train as a counsellor of female rape victims. Ms Nixon was referred to as 'she' in quotation marks. What rape victims would expect, the writer argued, was counselling from 'women who have suffered similar experiences, not from a man in a dress'.

The writer similarly applauded a judge's decision in Britain to reject a claim of sex discrimination brought against a pub landlord by five male-to-female transsexuals 'only one of whom had disposed of his meat and two veg'. She criticised the Equal Opportunities Commission for supporting the claimants and agreed with the judge, who said that, while he respected their wish to be regarded as women, a person's wish (apparently quoting the judge directly) 'doesn't determine what he is'.

Further into the piece there was a reference to Kwik-Fit sex changes, and the injunction to 'think about a world inhabited just by transsexuals. It would look like the set of Grease.' The column concluded: 'To go back to my five men and a toilet, I don't have a problem with men disposing of their genitals, but it does not make them women, in the same way that shoving a bit of vacuum hose down your 501s does not make you a man.'

The column attracted about 200 letters, nearly all of which I have read. There was clearly an international lobby at work but this by no means accounted for all the mail. All but four or five of the letters were condemnatory of the views expressed in the column. Many of them condemned the publication of the piece.

They also criticised the caricature illustration used with the column – a hairy-chested tattooed figure in a dress with a badge reading 'I'm a lady.'

Most of the letters went directly to Weekend, which published four of them – all critical of the column – the following Saturday. Some later correspondents felt that freedom of expression had thus been reasonably exercised. One wrote, '[Julie Bindel's] diatribe about transsexuals was unbelievably insensitive, but nevertheless she had a perfect right to express her thoughts, and to suffer the resulting slings and arrows.'

About a dozen letters came to me in the form of complaints. Some readers also made it clear that they were complaining to the Press Complaints Commission. The complaints were broadly that the article poured gratuitous offence on the members of a minority who already suffered discrimination and sometimes physical attack; that it showed not just a lack of sympathy but a lack of understanding of the experience of a transsexual person; that the language used by the writer tended to reinforce stereotypical views of transsexual people and thereby to encourage others to treat them with disdain or even hatred.

The editor of Weekend said: 'We [run] vigorous, opinionated and provocative columns on a whole range of subjects and this is something I'm keen to continue and protect ... There are very many times that we disagree with our columnists, sometimes vociferously, but that is not the point – we are not looking for consensus.

'In this case, we thought that what Julie Bindel was writing was particularly interesting because it came from her – a lesbian activist for the rights of women and children ... She is a rare kind of writer who puts her money where her mouth is.'

Julie Bindel said that writing in a different place and at greater length the tone might have differed and the piece itself have been more analytical. 'I know that lots of those wishing to go through sex change are deeply troubled and suffer discrimination.'

However, she would still say that was not the solution. 'We have invented a solution to a problem that we still do not really understand.'

Dismay at the piece was registered not only by transsexual people but also by doctors, therapists, academics and others involved in the field. One therapist wrote: 'Transgendered people would like to go about their lives in peace and dignity.' This column, which obscured any argument in discriminatory language, would not help them to do that. It abused an already abused minority that the Guardian might have been expected to protect.

February 14 2004

Humour and the bad taste test

Here is a joke that has been circulating in the medical profession about Alzheimer's disease. What does the patient get if you prescribe Aricept (brand name of one of the drugs now used to stabilise the symptoms of the disease) and (the anti-impotence drug) Viagra? Answer: A night to remember.

This is actually a version of a joke now so old that it has been held up as a classic. It was chosen as one of the '75 funniest jokes of all time' according to a poll conducted for American GQ, among comedians and comedy writers. We reprinted this in our news digest supplement, the Editor, on May 28. 'A man goes to the doctor. The doctor says, "I have bad news, and I have worse news. The bad news is you have Alzheimer's. The worse news is you have inoperable cancer and you'll be dead in two months." The man says, "Well at least I don't have Alzheimer's."'

A reader who has a spouse with Alzheimer's wrote to object to that joke. She said: 'You should know that Alzheimer's disease is not a mildly amusing case of forgetfulness in old age but involves the loss of so much that defines us as people: the ability to make relationships, to read, even to speak, loss of control over basic self care and even over bodily functions.'

The repetition of the joke in the magazine prompted the reader to write directly to me asking me to explain, 'where offending those whose brains are disintegrating and their carers comes in your hierarchy of concern'. One other reader wrote to complain about a version of the joke that referred to Ronald Reagan.

I was curious to know what my colleagues thought so I circulated the Reagan joke in the Guardian office, with the following questions: Did you laugh at this? Were you offended? Would you have published it?

About 35 replied. A small majority did not find it funny, most because it was a hairy old (and some said tasteless) gag. Only three were personally offended, but when it came to the question of publication almost a third would not have used it because they felt that the offence to others was very easily anticipated and should have been avoided. However, a majority still thought it was all right to publish.

Several of those who were uncomfortable with it did not like the fact that it was directed at an individual. I did not like that either. A couple said, try it this way: 'Iris Murdoch goes to the doctor's ...' Or put in the name of a relative who has Alzheimer's. The humour, someone suggested, quickly evaporates.

The most interesting result from this random survey was the discovery among the 35 or so who responded, of seven colleagues who had all cared or were caring for a close relative with Alzheimer's. Every one in this group defended the publication of the joke and the therapeutic value of humour to patients and carers.

One colleague said, 'I really think that faced with a loved one suffering from Alzheimer's or senile dementia, as I am with my mother, the best thing you can do is laugh ... She now has maybe 2% of her old life left to her yet she still has moments of enjoyment and laughter.' Another, who described the most taxing state of affairs, said, 'If you make light of the situation, it doesn't mean you don't care or love them, or that they are no longer the person you remember.'

The reader who complained to me suggested I spoke to Linda Grant, who has written about her mother's Alzheimer's and who, on Wednesday, wrote in G2 about another person with the disease. Grant told me, 'I think the black humour that surrounds this disease is often the only way it is made bearable for family and even people who have it.' She said the head of residential service at the home which looks after her mother had told her that he thought the most helpful book for relatives would be a joke book.

Before I forget, the joke that I began with. I had that from the chief executive of the Alzheimer's Disease Society. He said quite a lot of carers complained about Alzheimer's jokes, feeling that they trivialised things. But jokes, he added, undoubtedly had a role in coping and caring.

I went back to the reader who had complained. She said she felt this one had been laughing at, not with. Then she added, jokes OK, but please don't print crap ones.

July 10 1999

12.

CHOOSING THE WORDS

This section includes just one from several columns on the use of
four-letter words, all of them written – the columns that is – with
a certain amount of anguish. During my tenure as readers' editor
very good guidelines were devised for the use of what here I am
coyly going to call the F-word and C-word. The guidelines
attempted the difficult feat of recognising the prevalence of the
words in society at large while at the same time acknowledging
the sensibilities of readers who were offended by them. Perhaps
balance is impossible to achieve in this area. I was often
reminded of the punchline of a joke about a tightrope-walking
parrot brought home by a seafaring son of the vicarage. When a
titter ran through the audience on the parrot's first
demonstration at afternoon tea the bird paused on the tightrope,
turned towards the onlookers and said, 'Ludicrous perhaps, but
F-ing difficult.'

The words are often used regardless of the guidelines and do
not do much for the upward motion of circulation. The figures
recording the incidence of the words in the sample column below
are still roughly accurate. A plateau appears to have been
reached with a total over the past three years (I mean up to the
end of 2006) of 700 to 770 articles per annum in which the F-
word is used (an average of 2.5 articles an issue); and a more
modest total for the C-word, which occurs on average in one

article a week. The question here, and I believe it is quite a big one, is: are we simply noting their occurrence or promoting it?

All the columns here show how important readers consider our use of terminology and language in general to be. Was it appropriate to use the term 'ground zero' in a context that seemed to some readers to imply a lack of recognition of the magnitude and legacy of 9/11? Other columns look at the casual use of terms such as 'practising homosexual', 'schizophrenia' and its derivatives – now banned in so far as that is possible outside its proper medical context – and 'nutter'. Is it racist to describe those who transport drugs inside their bodies as a 'mule'? Does it compound the damage done by a racist outburst to report the use of the word 'nigger' spelling it out in full? Sometimes there are political implications, for example in calling Ukraine in its post-Soviet independent state 'the' Ukraine. I am with readers who see that language can break down prejudice or it can reinforce it. If you are a journalist then the choice is yours.

'Ground zero' as a benchmark

The Guardian's art critic, writing about a recent, disastrous fire at an art warehouse in east London, said: 'A rumour circulating yesterday suggested that Saatchi has been trying to buy the site, though one can't imagine exactly why, and it is being talked of as Brit Art's [sic] ground zero.' The headline asked: 'Is this Britart's ground zero?'

Several readers complained about what they regarded as an inappropriate and disproportionate use of the term ground zero. Some managed to do that without disparaging the work that had been destroyed. 'I was utterly gobsmacked to read this headline … It's just an awful, horribly insensitive thing to write. Congratulations to your arts team for being self-obsessed, divorced from reality and quite irritating,' wrote one reader.

One or two could not resist the temptation: 'It is a possible nadir in Guardian headline writing to compare the loss of thousands of innocent lives in an unprovoked terrorist attack with the loss of some laughably poor and much-derided so-called works of art in a fire. Have we forgotten how valuable human life is?'

The reference is, of course, to the site of the twin towers in New York. The term has been appropriated to apply to the focal point of the events of September 11 2001. According to the 1972 supplement to the Oxford English Dictionary, it originally belonged to a calamity of even greater magnitude, the dropping of the atomic bomb on Hiroshima. The dictionary defines ground zero as 'that part of the ground situated immediately under an exploding bomb, especially an atomic one'.

The first use it records is from the New York Times of July 7 1946: 'The intense heat of the blast started fires as far as 3,500 feet from "ground zero".' The dictionary gives one other reference, to a scientific bulletin of 1955: 'There was no noticeable contamination even at ground zero at Hiroshima.'

Since the attack on the twin towers, it has been used in the Guardian in relation to Hiroshima or to convey the scale and/or enormity of an event or situation. It was used in relation to the Bali bombing. It has been used to refer to the HIV crisis in China, to large-scale poverty in North Dakota, and to refer to Mississippi as America's 'ground zero of obesity'.

References in the US have covered a spectrum of taste. A Google search quickly discovered – among more than a million uses of the term – an illustrated advertisement for the 'Ground Zero thong', with the image of a man falling headlong on the front. This was from a range of goods aimed at skydivers.

Several US companies that have ground zero in their titles have felt it appropriate to put a note on their websites. One begins: 'We want to acknowledge the unfortunate coincidence between our organisation's name and what has become the descriptive term for the disaster site in New York City. We have discussed changing our name, but have decided against it. We would like to share our reasons for this and invite you to respond with your thoughts and concerns when you have finished reading.'

This company provides a focal point for people to collaborate on projects aimed at improving the urban environment and cultural life of Pittsburgh. The note on the website continues: 'In Pittsburgh, the phrase ground zero has become synonymous with creativity, community, and positive change. In our small way, we hope our use of the name will become something akin [to] a glimmer of hope and renewal where all hope seemed lost.'

Within six months of the attack on the twin towers, American teenagers, according to the Washington Post (quoted in the Editor section of the Guardian), had adapted the terminology of the 'war on terrorism' to the description of their own lives. Thus, it was reported, a student who had been disciplined suffered 'a total jihad' and a messy bedroom became, you have probably guessed, 'ground zero'.

The term was not used in relation to the Britart fire without some discussion. One suggestion considered and discarded was that it be used as the G2 cover line. In the event, it was used only with the art critic's commentary on page 5 of G2, where it was felt to be justified as the critic was reporting that this was what people were saying. The critic himself, I thought it was pretty clear, was trying to illustrate opposing poles of opinion, between those expressing schadenfreude (exuberant philistinism, you could say) and those who saw it as the disaster that it was. It was an overstatement, of course, because of the main associations of the term, but an understandable one.

June 5 2004

Life without the asterisk

Two stories on the front page of the Guardian on successive days last month in which unexpurgated expletives were used once again focused attention on the paper's policy on offensive language. One story involved the language and behaviour of the owner of the Daily Express, Richard Desmond, at a meeting with executives of the Daily Telegraph. The other was concerned with racist comments which led to the resignation from ITV of Ron Atkinson and the curtailment of his work for the sports pages of the Guardian.

In both stories the offending words were spelt out. One reader called on the day the Desmond story was published to register his strong objection to the use of the word 'fuck' in the story and to say he was cancelling his Guardian.

Both of these stories, in fact, fell within the Guardian guidelines and the publication of the spoken expletives in both cases was in my view justified.

This is not so with some of the occurrences which now appear in clear breach of the guidelines and which often attract complaint. One journalist said the proliferation of the words in the Guardian sometimes reminded him of the Flanders and Swann song: 'Ma's out, Pa's out, let's talk rude! Pee Po Belly Bum Drawers ...'

In the past year the F-word appeared in 722 stories in the Guardian, divided almost equally between the main broadsheet part of the paper and its supplements. The C-word – to which many of the paper's own journalists as well as readers take strong exception – appeared in about 70 stories.

The editor's guidelines say: 'Remember the reader – respect demands that we should not casually use words that are likely to offend. Use such words only when absolutely necessary to the facts of a piece, or to portray a character in an article; there is almost never a case in which we need to use a swear word outside direct quotes. The stronger the swear word, the harder we ought to think about using it. Never use asterisks, which are just a cop-out.' There is also a caution against the use of swear words in headings.

I sought the opinion of Guardian journalists with the following email: 'It is pretty clear that the guidance in the style guide is being widely ignored. The F-word is three times more likely to be encountered in the Guardian than in the Independent, the C-word is four times more likely to be met in the Guardian than the Independent. The words hardly ever or never occur in the other papers, broadsheet or tabloid. Is the Guardian's attitude OK? Too slack? Or should any attempt at control be abandoned (should the guidelines be scrapped?) Is the Guardian right to spell the words out? Or should it revert to the common convention of asterisks as in f***?'

About 100 journalists replied, of whom only 10 favoured the use of asterisks. One said: 'For some parents with young families, those trying to teach their kids about appropriate language and behaviour, it presents a problem: a paper they like and respect becomes the equivalent of a person they're wary of letting into the house, one who might use foul language in front of the kids.'

The overwhelming opinion, however, was strongly against the use of asterisks. 'Fuck is one of the commonest words in British demotic speech. Asterisks are silly and genteel and merely make the paper look fussy – they are the equivalent of Hyacinth Bucket [a character in a popular TV series who pronounced the name "bouquet"].' About half of the respondents to my email said the use of asterisks would be retrograde, patronising and coy. One said: 'The paper should reflect the way people use language in the real world.'

The editor of the Guide, which regularly attracts complaints, said: 'When I started editing in 2000, I was amazed at the coarse language people use quite casually in copy ... Now I find myself, with a roster of youngish writers covering popular culture, trying to negotiate some sort of taste line that allows for funny, frank and unfusty writing without being gratuitously offensive. I'm not sure you can get a uniform tone that pleases every age and social group – unless you just go for neutral with a blanket ban.'

No one wants that. A couple of people believed the guidelines should be abandoned because they were plainly not working and the whole thing should be left to the discretion of individual section editors.

Some thought the guidelines should be more stringent. More than half the journalists thought the guidelines were good and would still allow the paper to recognise changes in society if they were more vigorously applied. That is my view, too.

May 8 2004

The N-word

Several days ago the Guardian carried two pieces about a racist outburst at a Los Angeles comedy club by the actor Michael Richards, who formerly played Kramer in the television show Seinfeld. One was a news report on the international pages of the main paper by its Los Angeles correspondent, Dan Glaister. This was headed: 'Seinfeld actor lets fly with racist tirade'. The text spelled out the word 'nigger', used repeatedly by Richards in a sustained rant at a heckler (a black man) lasting some two minutes. The word was also picked up in the caption to an accompanying picture of Richards who, it said, 'was filmed calling black audience members "niggers"'.

The other article was a personal piece by Joseph Harker, the editor of the Guardian's Response column, who is black. This appeared in the features section G2 under the heading 'Nothing to laugh about in Kramer's N-word routine'. By agreement between Harker and the G2 editors, the word appeared with asterisks: n*****. Harker strongly believes that there are no circumstances in which the word should be spelt out and this view was respected in the treatment of his G2 opinion piece. I think that was the right thing to do.

This created an apparent anomaly, noted by several members of the Guardian staff in a poll I conducted, to which I am coming, in which Harker quoted, unasterisked, Richards's use of the word 'fucking', followed almost immediately by 'n*****'. The Guardian's guidelines on the F- and C-words say that when it is felt to be necessary to quote their use then they should be spelt out. In those circumstances the use of asterisks, in the editor's words, is a cop-out. However, I agree with Harker who has argued, as others have, that there is a significant distinction between the effect, the weight and the history of those words and the use of the word to which he so strongly objects.

He said: 'The fact is, it is different – and it is also different to the many other racial insults there are against black people. Its history is rooted in slavery and it comes with a message of white supremacy and black humiliation which is still very much alive today.' Harker used this argument against the use of the full word. My colleague Murray Armstrong, who is white, the person who most frequently deputises for me, acknowledged this history in very similar terms but came to the opposite conclusion.

He said, 'To argue that we should report what our headline described as a "racist tirade" without allowing our readers full knowledge of the language used underestimates their sensibilities and their ability to make ethical judgments, and diminishes the force and importance of the story.'

This is one of the very rare occasions when we are considering an issue raised not by readers – none has complained about either of these pieces – but by journalists here. There was a vigorous discussion at the editor's morning conference on the day of publication. I was not present but circulated an email to all Guardian editorial staff asking for their views on the use of the word 'nigger' in the news report. Almost 100 responded, not all of them journalists, supporting the treatment of the main news story by a ratio of more than 10 to 1. By no means all of the black or Asian journalists were among those who felt the treatment had been wrong or, drawing a further distinction, not all the black journalists thought it was wrong. Gary Younge, who has written eloquently on the specific subject in the past, told me, 'I don't think it should ever be used in headlines but my personal feeling is that when it is central to the story we have to use it ...' It should always be kept in mind, he felt, that it was so deeply offensive, but that did not mean it could never be used at all – particularly when it was central to the story. However, in this case, he said, once would probably have been enough.

The treatment here was carefully considered from start to finish. Dan Glaister said: 'None of the American media were using the N-word. The practice regarding use of such terms in the media here is much more cautious. The LA Times reported that Richards used a "racially offensive remark" before quoting other parts of his tirade ... I felt that hearing – or reading – the language was integral to understanding the crass and extreme nature of his remarks.'

It may be that some specific guidelines are required to ensure that the term never occurs in the Guardian outside a context that renders it necessary, as I believe the context on this occasion did.

Gary Younge's column on the subject appeared on January 7, 2002

November 25 2006

Misuse of mental health terms

Today is World Mental Health Day. Don't expect this to be immediately obvious. We did draw attention to it – but rather discreetly – in an excellent piece by Dr Lynne Friedli of the Health Education Authority in our Society section on Wednesday this week.

The designation of a special day is meant to encourage us to pause and examine our prejudices, and certainly the Guardian is not free from them. We stand in relation to some aspects of mental health – particularly in the way we refer to mental illness, in the language that we use and misuse – roughly where we stood in relation to race say 20 or 30 years ago.

An article by a student in the Guardian Higher Education supplement on Tuesday this week began: 'All students are schizophrenics ...' This prompted the following from a reader in Bristol: 'Why are you continuing to perpetuate this demeaning misuse of the term "schizophrenic", which refers to a very specific and serious psychiatric disorder ...?

'This is representative of the lazy and inaccurate use of many psychiatric terms, which does absolutely nothing for serious discussion of mental health issues and, if anything, makes it harder to have such discussion by distorting and misrepresenting major illnesses.'

The letter is one among many on this theme that I have received in the past few months, and it would be unfair to dwell on it. It does not draw attention to the worst of our transgressions, and it is not as if others are difficult to find. In the past year, the terms schizophrenia, schizophrenic, and schizoid have occurred in the Guardian 150 times, the majority of them in non-medical contexts, in effect perpetuating the split personality, or Jekyll and Hyde association – something we should all have abandoned as nonsense.

Thus we've been told that Radio 1 is 'deeply schizophrenic', that Serbia is suffering from 'economic schizophrenia', that 'Schizophrenia mounts at Middlesbrough' (not a health scare but a headline on a football preview), and we have even been assured (in our Society section!) that pharmaceutical companies are 'schizophrenic about genetics'.

All these sloppy or even flippant uses help to obscure a reality that others have learned to endure without much help from us. Indeed, it may be said that in some ways we exacerbate their difficulties. One person with whom I've had some correspondence about this is Dr Tom Harrison, secretary to West Midlands InSight, a group of people involved in mental health services who seek 'to encourage the media to promote accurate and respectful messages about the issues of mental ill-health'.

He writes: 'For most people who experience schizophrenia in this country, this is a tragic and alienating experience. Like all such experiences, with humility, hard work and much soul-searching, a number of people emerge with increased dignity and courage which I can only describe as a greater depth of humanity others do not. The closest parallel that I know of is the hostage experience.'

Dr Harrison objects to the way in which those who suffer, or who have suffered, from schizophrenia are described as 'schizophrenics' in a way that suggests this is the only thing that need be said about them. Those of us who know someone who suffers from schizophrenia are already aware that this is wrong and offensive.

Our social services correspondent, David Brindle, believes there should be a general tightening up of this kind of language and usage in the paper. I would go further, and say that we should stop using these terms altogether in non-medical contexts, and then to make sure we are using them accurately.

Particular care needs to be taken in coverage of violent crime where mental illness appears to be a factor. It is here that the worst excesses of language occur. You would not know from the dominance of this form of newspaper coverage, as someone writes to point out, that while recorded violent crime among the general public has increased greatly in the past 30 years, there has been no increase in violence by people with mental health problems.

There is now a great deal of cautionary advice available for journalists, from the Press Complaints Commission, the National Union of Journalists, the Schizophrenia Media Agency, and others. I have chosen to look just at schizophrenia, but we are wobbly in our references to all forms of mental illness.

A newspaper like the Guardian should be actively working to eradicate the stigma attached to mental illness. Is that what we are always found to be doing? No. Quite often we seem to be acting like a brake. The advice Kurt Vonnegut received from his father was sound: 'We're here to help each other get through this thing, whatever it is.'

October 10 1998

Inappropriate definitions of sexuality

The following brief item appeared in the Guardian a little over a week ago: 'Canon Jeffrey John, a prominent Church of England advocate of blessing gay marriages and the ordination of practising homosexuals, was named yesterday as the new suffragan bishop of Reading.'

The phrase 'practising homosexuals' brought, as it almost always does, protests from readers. I quote from some of those I have received over the past couple of years: '"Practising" to me implies some sort of trade or occupation rather than anything connected to sexual orientation. Although I don't suppose any Guardian correspondent is a raging homophobe, it is the sort of language used by people who are ... Could you not ask [journalists] to avoid it? It offends lots of decent people and doesn't seem to add anything in terms of meaning to the word "homosexual" or, preferably, "gay".'

Another reader wrote: 'You have written before on sensitivity around language in relation to ethnicity, religion, physical difference, and mental illness, for example. Your writers need to show more sensitivity around gay identity and relationships. Practising is not a word I can recall reading about heterosexuals. Gay people don't need to practise sex. We either have sex or we don't, just like heterosexual people.'

These arguments have been listened to and accepted, and a note was inserted in the style guide at least two years ago. Readers, and journalists, were reminded of it in a correction this week: 'The style guide is unequivocal on this point: Practising homosexual – do not use this grotesque expression.'

This created a problem for the paper's religious affairs correspondent, who sent me the following note: 'Although I didn't have anything to do with the brief on 'practising homosexuals' referred to in today's corrections, I do think it's worth a comment

– and perhaps consideration for our house style for future reference ... The point is that the churches do make a differentiation between people who are homosexual and those who are engaged in active sexual relationships ... The churches even recognise that homosexuals may become priests – where they draw the distinction is in whether they practise homosexuality or not. You can, in other words, be homosexual and a priest so long as you are celibate – just as if you're a Catholic priest you can be heterosexual so long as you don't have sex.

'The churches all draw the line at the practice of homosexuality; this is the whole significance of [the Archbishop of Canterbury] Rowan Williams's admission that he knowingly ordained a priest whom he knew to be practising – ie in a sexually active relationship. That is the condition that all the churches deem to be sinful or immoral. Therefore, there is a perfectly legitimate, indeed essential, qualification to be made here on the churches' position, or any bishop's position, on ordaining gays. This is the whole point of the Church of England and the Catholic church's policy. You cannot make sense of the religious debate without making this qualification and ... we absolutely need to continue making it ... In this case, at least, [the style guide] is categorically wrong-headed.'

The editor of the style guide was consulted and here is part of his note to the religious affairs correspondent: 'I take your point about the church's definitions but they never use the term "practising heterosexual" to describe a straight priest who has lapsed, do they? To me this term is clearly homophobic and the way round the problem is to refer to sexually active priests, whether gay or straight.'

The same colleague also told me, 'I feel it is important we follow this style and the sub who was responsible for the nib [news in brief] should have known better. It's been in the style guide for a long time and I have now reminded everyone of that.'

Our religious affairs correspondent is not convinced. 'I think any circumlocution is unfortunate not only because it adds unnecessary words – 'engaged in a homosexual relationship' as opposed to 'practising homosexual' – but also because it obscures and may falsify meaning (what about a priest engaged in casual gay sex? What about a priest in a stable long-term celibate relationship?).'

The paper, in my view, should seek to avoid the phrase. If and when the Anglican church uses it we should make it clear that we are quoting. The church's document, Issues in Human Sexuality, 1991, refers to 'homosexual practice', but it nowhere uses the specific phrase 'practising homosexual'.

May 31 2003

The reporting of race

I have been looking at two complaints dealing, broadly, with the reporting of race. One concerned the publication, on January 10 2004, of the photograph of a Kenyan man who had died as a result of Aids. The other concerned the use of the term 'mules' to describe drug couriers, particularly when applied to Jamaican women.

The first complainant said he would boycott the paper unless he was given an acceptable reason for the use of the picture of the dead man. He saw it as an example of what I described on a previous occasion as the prejudice of distance, although he did not use that term. 'What you cannot get away with in your own country or culture should not be an issue to play with when it relates to other cultures,' he said. Would we, he asked, publish a picture of a dead white person?

The question has been asked and discussed before. In fact, the Guardian has used pictures of dead white people in Northern Ireland, in former Yugoslavia, and in Zimbabwe, for example. On each occasion the particular circumstances have been considered.

A Guardian journalist who has reported extensively on Aids in Africa told me: 'Obviously it goes without saying that we must not show a dead black man if we would not show a dead white man in a similar situation in this country. If Aids were taking as devastating a toll in the UK as it is doing in sub-Saharan Africa, I think it is fairly safe to say that we would indeed be showing pictures of white people who have died ... I'm not against the use of pictures of the dead – black or white – if they are powerful images that move the reader, enhance understanding of the story and are acceptable to the family.'

The story in this case was about the way in which a cultural custom requiring the family of a dead person to cater for mourners on a comparatively lavish scale was imposing ruinous burdens. The increased frequency of death due to Aids was a significant exacerbating factor in a town, described as the poorest in Kenya, in a province with the country's highest rate of HIV.

The photograph, taken independently of the written report, showed Jarred Apamo in his coffin, with his youngest daughter looking through a window in the raised lid. He had died in Nairobi as a result of Aids and been taken back for burial in the same part of western Kenya, the home of the Luo people, from which the Guardian report was filed. The photographer, who has been living and working in Kenya for 18 years, had followed the body on this last journey with the full cooperation of Mr Apamo's family.

The assistant picture editor who selected the photograph said, 'If we had run a story on funerals in Ireland, Spain or Italy, where caskets are often open, we might have used a very similar picture.'

In the circumstances I hope the reader who complained will come to share my view that the use of the picture was appropriate and justified.

The second complainant objected to the term 'mules' as 'dehumanising and sexist'. Her complaint was prompted by the repeated incidence of the term in recent Guardian articles about Jamaican women who were used for the purpose of smuggling heroin, usually by swallowing it in latex wrappers.

She addressed her complaint initially to the journalist who had written two of these articles. In her letter, she acknowledged the attention paid to 'the political and social circumstances' of the women but objected to, and called for the complete abandonment of, the 'deeply offensive' label 'mules'.

In fact, these particular articles were very clearly concerned with the desperate circumstances of the women who were driven to act in this role and with the 'devastating' effect on their families and communities. In one of the pieces the journalist visited Jamaica to look at the contributory causes. At the time of her writing (October 2003) the 450 Jamaican women serving sentences after conviction for carrying wraps of cocaine in their bodies accounted for more than 10% of all foreign women in prison in Britain.

The term 'mule' in the Guardian has been applied not only to women, but to men, and to both black and white people. According to the Oxford English Dictionary, it has been used in connection with drugs since at least 1935.

In the examples I have looked at it has almost always been used in a context that would imply sympathy for the people to whom the term, in the sense we understand it, was accurately applied. The negative effect of frequent repetition should, however, be considered.

January 17 2004

Asylum without prejudice

A report on April 16, under the heading 'Migrants' 96 hours in police cells', was wrong to use the term 'bogus asylum seekers', both in the text and in a subheading. Its use is contrary to the paper's practice and journalists are warned against it in the style guide, although that particular term is not specified.

One or two people called to point out the lapse – complaints facilitated by the publication of the style guide on the paper's website. However, before any calls were received, the matter had been raised at the editor's morning conference and acknowledged as a mistake. Closer attention was promised.

The guidelines say in part: 'Asylum seeker – Someone seeking refugee status or humanitarian protection; there is no such thing as an "illegal asylum seeker".'

Although it is unstated, and perhaps should be spelled out, there is no significant distinction between the terms 'illegal asylum seeker' and 'bogus asylum seeker'. They are both wrong and to be avoided.

A very good leaflet offering guidance on terminology – in the process of being distributed to Guardian journalists – says on this point: 'Who is an "illegal asylum seeker"? No one. The term is always incorrect. It cannot be illegal to seek asylum since everyone has the fundamental human right to request asylum under international law. The term "bogus asylum seeker" is also inaccurate and misleading as it prejudges the outcome of an asylum application – rather like describing a defendant as entering a "bogus plea of innocence" during a trial.'

The leaflet is produced by MediaWise for the ethics council of the National Union of Journalists, with support from the United Nations high commissioner for refugees. MediaWise is the recently formed arm of the charity PressWise Trust, a change intended to indicate the extension of its interests beyond print journalism.

There is no divergence of responsible opinion on the subject. In October last year the Press Complaints Commission (PCC), recognising confusion in the media and among the public about the terms used to describe people claiming asylum, issued a note, saying: 'There can be no such thing in law as an "illegal asylum seeker". A "refugee" is someone who has fled their country in fear of their life, and may have been granted asylum under the 1951 refugee convention, or someone who otherwise qualifies for humanitarian protection, discretionary leave or has been granted exceptional leave to remain in the country. An asylum seeker can only become an "illegal immigrant" if he or she remains in the UK after having failed to respond to a removal notice.'

The Guardian's home affairs editor – who was not the author of the report that prompted this discussion – would like to see much more caution in the use of the term 'illegal immigrant', or better, its complete abandonment. 'Migrant', he suggests, would in many cases be a more accurate term than immigrant, which he says implies an intention of settling in the UK permanently: 'We often don't know what someone's intentions are and make too many assumptions.'

An asylum seeker, by his definition, is a migrant who makes a claim for refugee status. 'When a decision is made on the claim they either become a refugee, or somebody given humanitarian protection, or somebody given exceptional leave to remain (on compassionate grounds, for example), or a failed asylum seeker whose claim proved to be unfounded.'

When Article 19, the campaign for free expression, examined press coverage of the Sangatte Red Cross centre in northern France, it found 51 different labels used by journalists to refer to asylum seekers or refugees.

The home affairs editor again: 'In recent years "asylum seeker" has become a term of abuse and indeed in some newspapers it is just used as a euphemism for talking about race. The point is to try to restore some of the differences in meaning that these words are supposed to carry.'

To return to the PCC's note. It reminds journalists of the cautions against discrimination in clause 13 of its code, and adds: 'Similarly, the commission in previous adjudications under clause 1 (Accuracy) ... has underlined the danger that inaccurate, misleading or distorted reporting may generate an atmosphere of fear and hostility that is not borne out by the facts.' The terms we use need to be accurate and not prejudicial.

April 24 2004

Ukraine and the definite article

Ukrainian independence day is almost upon us – August 24 to be precise. But is the country Ukraine or 'the' Ukraine? The Collins dictionary, to which Guardian journalists are instructed to turn for guidance, says: 'Ukraine, the'. We only turn to Collins, however, when there is no relevant entry in the Guardian stylebook. In this case there is and it is very clear. It says: 'Ukraine, no "the".'

Every time we break this rule and refer to 'the Ukraine' we get objections. A Ukrainian reader writes: 'When will you finally stop using the offensive expression "the Ukraine"? The correct name of the country is "Ukraine".' On another occasion the same reader complained that use of 'the Ukraine' was 'patronising and colonial'.

On August 5 I put the following note in the daily corrections and clarifications column: 'The republic is Ukraine, not "the Ukraine".' The 'the' had been attached to it in an article in the Guardian's Saturday supplement Jobs & Money, where it said: 'Internet fraudsters from Russia, the Ukraine and the Baltic states were arrested in Britain by the hi-tech crime unit ...'

The Ukraine correction brought a protest from a reader, who wrote: 'I was rather irritated today to read the 853rd (approximately) grovel in the corrections and clarifications column for having followed perfectly normal English usage in writing "the Ukraine". Somebody (or bodies) seems to find this usage of the definite article offensive ... I can only wonder who the fuck is whining ...'

I replied: 'The Guardian stylebook says no "the". We follow the stylebook. The name of the country is not the Ukraine. It is Ukraine. The "the" for Ukrainians has echoes of imperial and Soviet dependence.' To make my own position clear: I am with the stylebook on this.

A historical note, courtesy of Collins, may be useful: 'Ukraine ... ruled by the Khazars (7th-9th centuries), by Rurik princes until the Mongol conquest in the 13th century, then by Lithuania, by Poland, and by Russia; one of the four original republics that formed the Soviet Union in 1922, unilaterally declared independence in 1990 which was recognised in 1991.'

Mikhail Heller and Aleksandr Nekrich in their book Utopia in Power, A History of the USSR from 1917 to the Present (Hutchinson, 1987), offer this explanation for the 'the': 'We know that there has been a historical hostility to the very idea of a separate Ukrainian nationality. Moscow's goal was to eliminate Ukraine and Ukrainians as political and cultural entities. Soviet translators, who knew the patterns for country names in English, deliberately translated the name of this area with the article 'the' because it then sounds to English-speakers like a part of a country rather than the name of an individual, independent country.

'Ukrainians who understood why Soviets were using the article "the" complained. In Russian, obviously, the word "Ukraina" has no article. Since the Soviet Union broke apart, Ukrainians have been pushing very hard to have the article 'the' removed from the English translation, so as to be linguistically correct, ie to show that Ukraine is a separate, independent country, not part of another country.'

The Oxford English Dictionary, in its definition of Ukrainian, points out that the word *ukraina* means border, frontier or marches, with connotations of edge or brink.

Nekrich and Heller are quoted in a website debate on the 'the' in country names (www.ezboard.com) where the extract, above, brought this response: 'This is just silly ... The Ukrainians, understandably want to have an English name that sounds like a "real" country, but the distortion of history in the service of nationalist pride is deplorable.'

The official website of Ukraine in its English language version refers to the country throughout as Ukraine. Even Nina Krushcheva, the granddaughter of Nikita Krushchev, referred to Ukraine as Ukraine, in a controversial article in which she asked: 'Does Ukraine have a history? Well, the place certainly does, but is the place a country? … It is more of a frontier than a region, let alone a country …'

Several months ago, the Guardian's stringer (freelance correspondent) in Berlin in a note on the struggle taking place in Ukraine to assert Ukrainian names in place of Russian, concluded: 'Also it's "Ukraine" (a country), not "the Ukraine" (a region of Russia).' Just so.

August 14 2004

Words that stereotype and stigmatise

Readers have written to my office in the past couple of weeks to complain about the use of several words that they argue are offensive and should be banned from intelligent discourse. One is 'nutter', and I quite agree with the complaint about that. Its general unacceptability was long ago recognised by the Guardian for very good reasons.

The word 'nutter' was used in a property column in the Weekend magazine of August 19 about Taggs Island on the Thames. 'I like islands,' the columnist wrote. 'They attract nutters.'

Surely, some readers (and some journalists) will say, there is nothing offensive about that. An eloquent complaint came from a reader who explained that he always enjoyed this property column – designed to help people planning to move – but, yet again, he said, the word 'nutter' had appeared in the paper and 'it (for me) besmirches the piece.' What the writer could have said, he suggested, was: 'I like islands. They attract eccentrics.' The fact that the word was clearly used in a light-hearted way made matters worse for this reader, helping to allow the word to remain for some, he argued, 'rather sloppily ... acceptable'.

'For those of us who have experience of mentally ill relatives, as I have (with my wife just having been released from a psychiatric hospital after a 20-week stay), and, indeed, to those unfortunate individuals (my wife is also a Guardian reader), the term is unequivocally offensive.' Is there a Guardian policy on the use of this word, he asked.

Yes, there is, and it is embodied in an entry in the style guide (available to all online) under the heading 'mental health'. This is what it says: 'Take care using language about mental health issues. In addition to such clearly offensive and unacceptable expressions as loony, maniac, nutter, psycho and schizo, terms to avoid – because they stereotype and stigmatise – include victim of, suffering from, and afflicted by; 'a person with' is clear, accurate and preferable. Never use schizophrenic to mean 'in two minds'. And avoid writing 'the mentally ill' – say 'mentally ill people ...'

I feel a strong commitment to this policy. It has nothing to do with political correctness. It has a lot to do with the way we treat each other, and in particular the way in which we relate to each other in times of need. The use of such terms disappoints readers who expect the Guardian to combat, not reinforce, tendencies in society that stigmatise and discriminate against people.

Advice and explanation are readily available to all journalists. I recommend a look at an article by Lynn Eaton headed 'Mind your language', published in Media Guardian on January 23 2006 (you can read it on the Guardian website by looking under the author's name and registering for free access to the media pages). It describes a five-year campaign, called Shift, aimed at reducing stigma and discrimination, conducted with the cooperation of the National Union of Journalists and the Society of Editors.

Shift's web address appears below. I quote from its home page: 'One in 6 people will currently be experiencing problems with their mental health. That means that even if you haven't experienced a mental health problem yourself, you almost certainly know many people who have. People sometimes feel that they need to keep their problems a secret because of the way that others treat them. The stigma that surrounds mental health can mean that people find it more difficult to get the job that they want or education that they need, even though some of our greatest politicians, academics, business brains and artists have proved that mental ill health need not be a barrier to success.'

This is the context in which to consider the depressing regularity with which the term 'nutter' still crops up.

August 28 2006

An inconclusive game of marbles

A week ago the Guardian carried a review by the former chairman of the BBC Gavyn Davies of the memoirs of the former director general of the corporation Greg Dyke. In it he said: 'Greg says that, in pursuing an illegitimate complaint, [Alastair] Campbell behaved like "a deranged, vindictive bastard", on the verge of losing a full set of marbles.'

The reference to marbles caught a reader's attention. 'What is the derivation of this phrase? Why should losing one's mind be associated with marbles?' In this particular case, the reviewer offered what amounted to an explanation and qualification of its meaning: 'In my view, Campbell has many admirable qualities, but was undoubtedly going through a bad patch which made life for the rest of us (the prime minister, for example) almost impossible.' The context is the angry turmoil attending the Andrew Gilligan affair.

It is not a phrase that crops up in the Guardian very often and it is usually used with a non-serious or jocular intent. One of its fairly rare appearances – almost five years ago – was in a headline that read: 'Why losing one's marbles isn't all bad'. The story was about the Elgin marbles.

The reader's query nicely coincided with the arrival on my desk of a new book by Nigel Rees, A Word in Your Shell-like: 6,000 Curious and Everyday Phrases Explained (Collins) – a treasury of stimulating excursions and digressions in the English language.

Rees actually explores but dismisses the association of the phrase with the Elgin marbles. 'At the popular level,' he says, 'most people believe the phrase derives from a joke. When Lord Elgin brought back his famous marbles from the Parthenon and they ended up in the British Museum in 1816, the Greeks were hopping mad (and, indeed, remain so). But, with all due respect and however entertaining, this is not an origin to be taken seriously.'

According to Rees, 'almost everyone' agrees that the expression is American in origin and he notes that the Oxford English Dictionary finds it first recorded in the journal American Speech in 1927. In fact, the OED (Supplement, 1976) provides the actual example from American Speech: 'There goes a man who doesn't have all his marbles.'

Rees explores the possible association of the phrase with the French *meubles*, 'furniture, movables' (which the OED describes as a false translation), and asks, 'Could one imagine "to lose one's marbles" coming from the idea of losing one's "mind furniture"?' He quotes in support two sayings that use furniture as an indicator of mental well-being or the lack of it. One is from a correspondent in Cheshire who notes there the expression, 'He's got all his chairs at home'; and one from a correspondent in Yorkshire who wrote, 'If someone is a bit lacking in the head, we say that they haven't got all their furniture at home.' Hence, Rees suggests, 'a home without furniture is empty, so "lost one's marbles" = empty-headed, no longer at home, no longer "there".'

One of the examples that he calls in support actually seems to me to argue an altogether more direct and plausible origin. It comes from a publication of the English Dialect Society (West Cornwall Words) in 1880: 'Those that have marbles may play, but those that have none must look on.' Rees says: 'Surely this admirably conveys the misfortune of those who are without the necessary wherewithal to participate in the game of life?'

So it does but, unless I am losing my marbles, it is simply making an illustrative reference to the game of marbles (for a history see www.marblemuseum.org). The OED cites references to the game from English sources from around the beginning of the 18th century. The OED Supplement, by the way, equates the word with mental faculties, brains, or common sense. Although it doesn't make the direct connection between the game and the use of the word according to that definition, none of the examples it quotes seem incompatible with the idea. To give a couple of them: 'Do men who have got all their marbles go swimming in lakes with their clothes on?' (PG Wodehouse's Cocktail Time, 1958); 'You lost your goddam marbles? You gone completely crazy, you nutty slob?' (John Wainwright's The Take-Over Men, 1969). Certainly not the sort of language we like to see in the Guardian.

Forgive me for digressing, but as I found while browsing in Nigel Rees's book, one thing leads to another and it's a short step from the sublime to the ridiculous.

October 2 2004

13.

THE ENGLISH LANGUAGE

If the use of English is considered as a single subject then it is easily the one that attracts most correspondence from readers. It has meant that when there is no pressing uproar over the Guardian's coverage of this or that the column has been able to plunge into consideration of such questions as: Should that be may or might? Is it a sin to split an infinitive? Is it all right to say alright?

A reader writes, 'Forgive me if this is over pedantic ...' Believe me, it isn't. Responding to this unremitting flow is always a great pleasure. It has enabled me to take restorative baths in the great Oxford English Dictionary and in all the other works of exploration, sometimes called reference books, that I hope you will find fully acknowledged here. There is nothing like a good dictionary. If you are writing news it guides you towards precision. If you are writing something other than news, then familiarity with the nuances of meaning and association of a word – and its history – should make your writing more lively and eventful and expressive on the page.

You cannot work for a newspaper and fail to be conscious of the fact that you are working with a living and changing language. To vary the words of the song: it is what you say and the way that you say it. A newspaper is an arena where battles for survival or acceptance are fought out. I can't tell you what a privilege it has been to have a ringside seat for the past decade. But perhaps I can.

Words that are open to interpretation

English, n. A language so haughty and reserved that few writers succeed in getting on terms of familiarity with it.

I find the company of Ambrose Bierce a great comfort in my lonely role of readers' editor. He was a satirical journalist, roughly a century ago, whose exasperation with the printed medium was clearly exacerbated by his daily reading in it. Time does not lessen my sympathy for him. So affected was he by the excesses and idiocies of the world of journalism, to which he belonged, that the effect was to stimulate the production of a series of scathing 'definitions' which still have the power to chasten while causing us to smile. (**Print, n.** Feathers, in which many sickly ideas strut about and crow, that had better never have been hatched.) I must stop lest my praise for him should appear fulsome.

The language that we use and misuse in the Guardian is a subject of intense interest to the paper's readers, who often try to help even while crying in pain. 'Please try to make (your colleagues) understand the difference between effect and affect. I am so affected by the numerous occasions of misuse that the effect is to make me want to scream.' Alas, so many casualties and so few ambulances (affect and effect, I feel obliged to remind you, were once confused in this column).

Fulsome is a particular black beast of mine (I would say *bête noire* but we notoriously misspell foreign terms, as readers of the corrections and clarifications column will have observed). Fulsome is one of those words we use, more often than not, in ignorance of its meaning. Here are just a couple of recent examples. 'All bar Japan had made fullsome (sic) commitment to deeper and wider debt relief' (from a leader of a few weeks ago). 'Media interest in the fulsome figure of actress Kate Winslet ...' Fulsome does not mean wholehearted and it does not mean ample or generously proportioned. It means, as the Guardian style guide, lying there and longing to be consulted, would have pointed out, cloying, excessive, disgusting by excess. So 'fulsome praise', the style guide very helpfully adds, should not be used in a complimentary sense.

Lying and laying cause constant trouble. The people we noticed 'laying on their backs' were, in fact, lying on their backs and we were laying another egg. Many of these things, they are too numerous, do not get into the daily corrections column. That column and this weekly Open Door column are complementary, although not always complimentary, two words defining a distinction that we sometimes fail to grasp, as we did in the wording of a recent advertisement for (appropriately enough) the Guardian.

Another word under siege, as you frequently point out, is enormity. It may be all right to say, as we did, '[Milosevic's] chances of survival will diminish as the enormity of the disaster he has brought on Serbia sinks in,' but is it all right to speak of 'some comic physical enormity a long nose or a bulbous crotch'? Perhaps. Again, the style guide is there for those willing to be helped: enormity, something monstrous or wicked, not synonymous with large.

Readers are not always right (I throw that in for colleagues who find the catalogue depressing). For example, the reader who suggested that a leader which began, 'The financial hurricane that wreaked such havoc' was wrong, was wrong herself. She thought we should have said wrought but wrought is the past tense of work not of wreak. We do not say wreaked iron because we have not inflicted havoc or chaos upon it.

We often appear to have difficulty in placing things comfortably in the past, saying sprung in place of sprang, sunk where we should say sank, but it is not wrong, as one reader suggested it was, to say (in a headline), 'Spin doctor who spun out of control'. Span, on the other hand, would have been wrong.

The point, however, is that you would like us to be accurate, both factually and in our use of language. The two go together, as in the following from the paper this week, 'An American embassy official confirmed that one of their subjects had been expelled.' A terse email from a professor of law at a university in Florida said: 'We do not have "subjects". We have "citizens".'

It does not seem unreasonable that you should demand we extend the curiosity with which we survey the world to the language we use in describing what we see. We sometimes launch ourselves into sentences as though embarking on a journey in completely unfamiliar country. We do not wish to be thought reliable only for our inaccuracy.

Accuracy, let's see how Mr Bierce defines it: A certain uninteresting quality carefully excluded from human statements.

I'll end there.

Ambrose Bierce: The Enlarged Devil's Dictionary is published by Penguin

July 24 1999

How to correctly use the English language

In my column last week about the Guardian's forthcoming change from the present broadsheet to the smaller Berliner format I split an infinitive. I did not notice until I read the printed column over on Saturday. You did not notice at all. You would have let me know.

Here is the sentence: 'A further £12m is being spent on all the ancillary equipment needed to, for example, turn computerised content into plates for the presses, handle the giant reels of newsprint, etc.' If I had stumbled when reading it over before publication I might have preferred to have said it like this: 'A further £12m is being spent on all the ancillary equipment needed, for example, to turn computerised content ...' That would have been better in all respects – and would certainly have avoided the dissonant clang. But splitting an infinitive is no longer regarded as a particularly serious offence, as it was when schoolchildren were routinely thrashed for getting it wrong (just joking).

A reader did write, not about this example but about another one, chosen from the many available. 'What is Guardian policy on that old favourite, the split infinitive?' he wanted to know. He pointed to a report in the Daily Telegraph in which the chairman of the BBC governors, Michael Grade, was said to be noted for 'hating split infinitives'. Then he turned accusingly to the following sentence in the Guardian on the same day: 'Last week's annual report by the ... governors [of the BBC] said they had asked management to further reduce the number of repeats.' What comes naturally, 'to further reduce' or 'to reduce further'? Or perhaps more to the point, which sounds more natural?

The Guardian stylebook is sensibly relaxed on the subject and introduces its entry by quoting from the first edition (1926) of HW Fowler's Modern English Usage: 'The English-speaking world may be divided into (1) those who neither know nor care what a split infinitive is; (2) those who do not know but care very much; (3) those who know and condemn; (4) those who know and distinguish.' Fowler then adds: 'Those who neither know nor care are the vast majority, and are happy folk, to be envied.'

I direct you to the couple of pages on the subject to be found in modern editions of the book. (If you are reading this column and don't have a copy you should certainly get one – you would enjoy it.) I have The New Fowler's Modern English Usage, the third edition, revised in 1998 by RW Burchfield, who starts with the categorical statement: 'No other grammatical issue has so divided the nation since the split infinitive was declared to be a solecism in the course of the 19th century.'

He then explains what is and what is not a split infinitive, using as an example 'to love'. To split the infinitive is to insert a word or words between the particle 'to' and the verbal part, 'love'. 'To madly love' is a split infinitive. 'My mother taught me to be always prepared,' is not ('to always be prepared' would be).

To return to the Guardian stylebook: 'It is perfectly acceptable to sensibly split infinitives, and stubbornly to resist doing so can sound awkward and make for ambiguity.' Just so.

Burchfield, assessing the situation in the last two decades of the 20th century, observed, 'There can be no doubt that there continues to be a noticeable reluctance to split infinitives both in the national press and in the work of many of our most respected writers.' However, he notes that the Times, in a leading article in 1992, said, 'The most diligent search can find no modern grammarian to pedantically, to dogmatically, to invariably condemn a split infinitive.'

The entry in this edition of Fowler, after stating that there should not be an absolute taboo, concludes by quoting from another book by Burchfield, The Spoken Word (BBC, 1981): 'Avoid splitting infinitives whenever possible, but do not suffer undue remorse if a split infinitive is unavoidable for the natural and unambiguous completion of a sentence already begun.'

These things can be therapeutic in troubled times. A correction for connoisseurs appeared in the regular daily column on Wednesday this week. We misplaced an apostrophe in the title of a book by Hannah Pool, a colleague here at the Guardian. The title is My Fathers' Daughter, not My Father's Daughter. It is about her two fathers, the one who raised her in Britain and her birth father in Eritrea. The whole point, you could say, was in the apostrophe.

July 30 2005

A long list of imperfections

One tries but one does not necessarily succeed. A couple of weeks ago I devoted this column to a reader's query about the pros and cons of splitting an infinitive, concluding that a strict taboo no longer applied. One reader wrote to say that the taboo had been abandoned so long ago that he was surprised to find me bothering with the subject at all. My time, he suggested, would be far better spent dealing with other aspects of Guardian English. He then listed a few quirks of particular annoyance to him.

One reader seemed to miss the point entirely, addressing himself to the headline on the column in which I had – rather cleverly I thought – split an infinitive. The heading read, 'How to correctly use the English language'. 'Please,' the reader shouted, 'How to use the English language correctly!' (his exclamation mark).

I know that some of you read beyond the headline because the column prompted an unusual amount of correspondence. One reader wrote to say it reminded her of a cartoon she had seen in the Times Educational Supplement 'in about 1976'. 'This showed a schoolboy bursting through a door marked Language Laboratory and saying to a teacher in the corridor, "Please sir, Blenkinsop's just split the infinitive!"'

Several readers reminded me of a remark attributed in various versions to George Bernard Shaw, who is said to have complained of an editor who tinkered with his infinitives: 'I don't care if he is made to go quickly, or to quickly go – but go he must' (that particular version comes from the Guardian stylebook).

Many thanks to the reader who sent the following extract from Raymond Chandler Speaking (University of California Press, 1962), a selection of the crime writer's correspondence. This is from a letter of January 1948 addressed to the editor of the Atlantic Monthly: 'Would you convey my compliments to the purist who reads your proofs and tell him or her that I write a sort of broken-down patois which is something like the way a Swiss waiter talks, and that when I split an infinitive, God damn it, I split it so it will stay split and when I interrupt the velvety smoothness of my more or less literate syntax with a few sudden words of bar-room vernacular, that is done with the eyes wide open and the mind relaxed and attentive. The method may not be perfect, but it is all I have.'

One reader argued, 'It is time this prejudice [against splitting infinitives] was buried, as should be the other pedant's idea that it is wrong to say that a preposition is something I should not end a sentence with.'

Nearly all the correspondents took the opportunity to raise other matters. 'Perhaps you could follow up your split infinitive column with one on the positioning of "only". Notwithstanding the clarity of your style guide on this tricky word, it is [almost always] misplaced (and frequently in the Guardian).' The stylebook says, 'Only – can be ambiguous if not placed next to the word or phrase modified: "I have only one ambition" is clearer than 'I only have one ambition.'

This reader said, 'I think wrong "onlies" annoy me more than split infinitives.' There is no getting away from these things. 'In my local underground car park,' he wrote, 'there is a notice on the wall saying "Parking for residents only on this level". This ambiguity can be interpreted to mean that residents must park on no other level other than this one and that non-residents may also park on this level. However, we know that what the sign actually means (or at least wants to say) is that this level is for residents only (indeed, only residents) and that non-residents must park on other levels.'

He concludes, 'I've never bothered to make a stand, as I would be arguing a finer point of grammar with a car park attendant without English as a first language.' A wise decision, if I may say so. Although, I speak as someone who will not cross the threshold of a shop or restaurant that misspells 'licensed'.

Occasionally, I feel that far from having a calming effect these columns trigger a bout of twitching. Subjects to which I am invited to turn my attention include: may and might (again), hung and hanged, less and fewer, and the apparent decline of 'different from' in favour of the appalling 'different than'.

I leave you with this thought, courtesy of a valued contributor: 'Care of and for the language is not only good for the soul (as music is) but prevents evil thoughts being propagated.' Thanks for that.

August 13 2005

Glimpses of something shocking

A reader writes from Whitstable: 'For three weeks running there have been words in the Guide that I don't understand and are not in my Concise Oxford Dictionary. Would you please define them for me and ask the people who write this stuff to be a bit more considerate towards those of us who don't move in their circles?'

Sometimes it is better not to ask. The words were doofus, Milf, and shibbying. The editor of the Guide offers the following: 'Doofus – affectionate slang for an idiot. In fairly wide currency [in the UK], although probably American in origin. Milf – a term popularised in the movie American Pie. A teenage acronym for an attractive older woman. Mother [or Mom] I'd like to …' Well, something beginning with F. You should have no difficulty with it if you are a regular reader of the Guardian. The editor of the Guide adds helpfully: 'Now I come to think of it, there is the more polite "yummy mummy". Shibbying – stoner slang, used in the film Dude, Where's My Car? It means get stoned/drunk. Eg "I shibby", "we shibbed", "that was some serious shibbying we did last night." Shibby as an adjective can mean cool. "They're a shibby band."'

On, or near, the subject of questionable language, a reader writes from Stocksbridge on the 'misuse' of the word expletive, or rather the tendency to confine it to the meaning that dictionaries give first – a swear word.

'An expletive is a purely decorative word that may be deleted without affecting meaning: hence in "Hark! Hark! The dogs do bark", the expletive "do" is present solely for the sake of scansion. The fact that expletives are often indelicate does not mean that an indelicate word is necessarily an expletive.' I am indebted.

Another reader writes: 'Given that the Guardian admirably offers corrections when it blunders, should we not expect equal attention to be given to the erroneous dissemination of incorrect linguistic information?' This reader wanted to take up discussion of the term 'square meal', which had, he insisted, contrary to what we had said, nothing to do with the shape of the plate on which it was served. 'Square [here] is cognate with honest, straightforward, and in the case of food, full, solid or substantial.'

The English language, particularly the Guardian's use of it, is of huge fascination to readers and forms the subject of much correspondence.

Aspects that some may regard as unsavoury are not shied away from by others, but generally treated with delicacy. '"Genius-come-role model" should of course be "cum", Latin "with",' wrote one reader. 'You may not wish to speculate on why this Anglicisation is becoming increasingly common – I suspect it's because "cum" as a misspelling of "come" has acquired a specific sexual meaning.' Which gives us a combined euphemism and homophone.

It is well to be conservative, but not too conservative. Words vary in meaning over time. Sensible concessions have to be made. A reader took exception to the use of the word 'electrocute' to mean 'accidental death from electric shock'. He did so because it was coined, he said, in the US in the early 20th century, as a deliberate compound of 'electricity' and 'execute'. 'It refers to the death met by people sentenced to the electric chair ... Why does this disgusting word remain in (mis)use?'

The first definition in Collins, the Guardian's default dictionary (the dictionary to which journalists are expected to turn when a meaning or usage is not covered by the paper's own style guide) is 'to kill as a result of an electric shock'. The second definition, associated with the US, is 'to execute in the electric chair'. The style guide recognises common usage and offers this note: 'electrocution – death by electric shock, so don't say survivors of torture were 'electrocuted' during their ordeal – rather that they were given electric shocks.'

The report to which the reader objected concerned the death of a woman in New York by accidental electric shock. It was a perfectly appropriate word to use in the circumstances. We use it to mean any death by electric shock and not to apply only to circumstances in which someone is executed or deliberately put to death by electric shock.

Is that alright? Is alright all right? No it is not. Alright still sneaks into the Guardian. The style guide says 'all right is right; alright is not all right'; a confused association with already, perhaps.

Thanks to Martin Elliott, Robin Dow, Jonathon Green, Jean Hill, Garrick Alder, Peter Kennedy.

February 21 2004

Persistent errors in the Guardian's English

The daily corrections and clarifications column was not really set up to handle mistakes in the Guardian's use of English, although it has had a 'homophone corner' almost since it began seven years ago. Rather than carry corrections or notes about our English there I have generally preferred to use this Open Door column, where I have the opportunity to quote your thoughts and ramble through the reference books.

Such is the weight of mail on the subject, however, that I feel under increasing pressure to include them in the daily corrections. This is particularly true in the case of persistent errors.

For example, on Wednesday this week, the corrections column contained the following note: 'Efforts to derecognise "led" as the past tense and past participle of "lead" continue, as in "Arthur Scargill, who lead his men" (from a leader of March 5); and "Badat lead the traditional Ramadan recitals …" (from a news report the same day).'

One of the readers who drew the first of these to my attention confined herself to a brief exasperated comment: 'Tense? Very.' Why is it such a persistent error? Does it have something to do with the fact that lead, the 'heavy bluish-grey soft ductile metallic element occurring naturally in galena and used in building and the manufacture of alloys' (Oxford) is pronounced led? Or that what we have in our pencils is lead (pron: led)?

Whatever the reason, the failure to recognise the legitimacy of 'led' as something we used to do afflicts some of the Guardian's leading columnists. To quote a couple of examples: 'Never has the EU been at such a low ebb, badly lead with too little vision'; and 'It has lead to a tenfold increase in arrests.' The affliction is clearly shared by some subeditors and editors.

There is no warning in the Guardian stylebook, which might,

perhaps, have been expected to take a lead in this as it has led and still leads in so many other ways. However, it is now in the online version.

Grammatical errors are interruptions that divert the reader from the content, even when the content is urgent or grave. A reader writes, quoting from an article in the Guardian this week: '"She was told she may never walk again after breaking her back in a riding accident." The confused tenses in this meant that I believed that [the person involved] still had a problem until I read the rest of the piece and was happy to find she is now OK. As always, wrong tense means lost sense – it should have read, "she might never walk again".'

The stylebook offers guidance that the writer might have found useful (had it been consulted): 'may or might? The subtle distinctions between these (and other so-called modal verbs) are gradually disappearing, but they still matter to many of our readers and can be useful.

'May implies that the possibility remains open: "The Mies van der Rohe tower may have changed the face of British architecture forever" (it has been built); Might suggests that the possibility remains open no longer: "The Mies tower might have changed the face of architecture forever" (if only they had built it). Similarly, "they may have played tennis, or they may have gone boating" suggests I don't know what they did; "they might have played tennis if the weather had been dry" means they didn't, because it wasn't.

'May also has the meaning of "having permission", so be careful: does "Megawatt Corp may bid for TransElectric Inc" mean that it is considering a bid, or that the competition authorities have allowed it to bid?'

RW Burchfield in The New Fowler's Modern English Usage (Oxford) is good and more extensive, even expressing some sympathy for those who struggle: 'I can see how easy it is to confuse the roles of 'may' and 'might' when in some circumstances they are more or less interchangeable.' He quotes the following from the Guardian of 1990: 'A mentally ill man may not have committed suicide had he been kept in hospital, rather than been discharged to be cared for in the community.' He says, 'Had the Guardian placed the headline "Mentally ill man may not have committed suicide" above [that] the reader would not have been certain whether the person concerned had, or had not, committed suicide ... until the text of the news item made it clear just what had happened.' Burchfield says that, in his view, 'may not have' in the Guardian text is wrong and that it should have been 'might not have'.

He may be right. I believe he is.

March 19 2005

The return of the apostrofly

Among the electronic sackfuls of hate mail emanating from the US a few weeks ago – we do not want to go into the reasons again [see Chapter 9] – was a terse communication that read, 'The Guardian is not a proper newspaper ... and you are not a proper journalist.'

This slur takes no account of my many achievements in almost 50 years of journalism. Obviously I cannot list them all in such a short column, but forgive me if I set my natural modesty aside for a moment to tell you of the main one.

This is the discovery of the apostrofly, first recorded in this column in the Guardian on September 30 2002. The apostrofly, as I noted at the time, is an insect which lands at random on the printed page, depositing an apostrophe wherever it alights.

The activities of this creature, by the way, were completely overlooked by Lynne Truss in her otherwise admirable book, Eats, Shoots & Leaves: The Zero Tolerance Approach to Punctuation (Profile). Rather naively, if I may say so, she clings to the idea that the apparently misplaced apostrophe is attributable to human failing.

Anyone can see that this is not the case. To take an example (from a recent edition of G2): 'This break's Kant's maxim ...' Clearly the work of the apostrofly. Similarly, no one would seriously suggest that the placing of the apostrophe in the following (from a recent letters page) was the work of a human hand: 'With reports that 100,000 Iraqi's ...'

I can claim to be solely responsible for the discovery of this creature. If you tap 'apostrofly' into Google it will come up with just 18 examples, all of them originating in my column of a couple of years ago. Not a proper journalist, indeed ...

To move to more serious matters raised by readers over the past few weeks. 'I would like to remind your journalists of the existence of the word "persuade". It seems almost entirely replaced by the cuckoo "convince". Surely the distinction between persuading someone to do something and convincing them of something is still valuable and should not be thrown away.' The reader reminds me, reminds us all, that, 'It has even been known that someone is persuaded, for instance to cast a vote, without being convinced.'

Here is a recent example from the Guardian which perfectly illustrates this reader's point: 'Through a friend, she managed to convince a wealthy Brooklyn family to let her sleep in their basement for a week.' This should clang painfully on your ear.

The misuse or even invention of verbs is a preoccupation. 'Your article on October 30 drew attention to the use of "showcase" as a verb (I could have said highlighted its use but I'm not sure anymore [sic, English use is any more; anymore is US English]) ... Now it seems any word at all can be used as a verb, or "verbed", possibly. The biscuit was finally taken when the Business Notebook, talking about the practice of relocating call centres abroad, introduced us to the word "offshoring". I nearly heart attacked. In the sports pages we hear from Olympic athletes expected to medal in their event so I can only hope that Manchester United facup again this year.'

Now, perhaps, he has gone too far. This brings me to the following protest at what another reader sees as overblown language in the Guardian, particularly in headlines: 'Would it be possible to create a hierarchy of words in descending order of magnitude with approximate definitions?' Could I not do something about overheated language, the reader asked, before it became a disaster, or catastrophe, or tragedy? Could we, perhaps, have some genuine, not journalistic sense of proportion?

This is, in fact, one of the aspects of the Guardian's journalism that is being discussed here as the paper moves towards its new midi or Berliner format: towards a calmer conversation between writer and reader.

A reader writes in reply to an email from me: 'As, ever, your tone is so sweetly reasonable that you are probably right. And yet …' He then went on to take issue over a number of points we have discussed before, almost (but not quite) to exhaustion: 'It really depresses me that Guardian readers do not see the value of distinguishing between [something] which is alright (that is acceptable), and [something] which is all right (that is correct in every particular).'

Another reader, also reluctant to bow to the Guardian stylebook, said, 'When in doubt, common usage is always correct. Language creates grammarians – grammarians do not create language.'

December 4 2004

A headline too far

Fowler, in his Modern English Usage (revised by RW Burchfield), third edition, 1998, is at his sniffiest on the subject. 'A regrettable tendency has emerged in recent years, especially in non-standard English in Britain and abroad, to construe the verb with of.' He is talking about the verb to bore, defined in James Murray's Oxford English Dictionary as 'to weary by tedious conversation or simply by the failure to be interesting'.

Fowler says: 'The normal constructions are with with or with by.' He, or rather his successor, Mr Burchfield, gives a number of examples of the (mis)use of the verb with 'of'. Remarkably, none is taken from the 200 or so occurrences in the Guardian over the past few years.

'I'm so bored of him. He's lost his virility' (C Phipps, 1989) is one of Burchfield's examples. He also quotes Iona Opie, 1993, presumably from her The People in the Playground: '[Children] use the preposition "of" in an unorthodox way: "I'm bored of this," they say (taking the construction from "tired of").'

I hope I am not boring you with this. Several of you always write when 'bored of' occurs in the text of a story. Last week rather more than several of you wrote. 'I noticed an article was topped by the headline "Bored of fashion". There seems to be an increased use of the word "of" to follow bored ... but this is the first time I have seen it used in a headline ... To me it always sounds wrong. Is it one of those things that used to be wrong but is now becoming acceptable because more and more people do it?'

No it is not acceptable (yet). The following appeared in the corrections and clarifications column: 'The headline "Bored of fashion", supported by a couple of similar references in the text, caused an understandable gnashing of teeth. The style guide says: bored with, by, not bored of. The confusion perhaps comes from the legitimate "tired of".'

It was not, in fact, the first time the construction had appeared in a headline. Here is a note from the corrections column just a year earlier: 'Language department: a headline "Adam Cooper left the Royal Ballet because he was bored of dancing the classics". The construction "bored of" is banned by our style guide, which, quite rightly, prefers bored with or by. (He was tired of dancing the classics and bored by doing so.)'

It is not just us or you. Quite a recent book, Mind the Gaffe: The Penguin Guide to Common Errors in English by RL Trask (2001), says: 'Bored – The established expression is bored with, not bored of, which should be avoided in careful writing.'

These are little things made bigger when they creep into headlines. Even so they rank very low on the scale of journalistic sins. Much more annoying for many of you are headlines based on cliche quotes: A man for all seasons; Not waving but drowning; A (something) too far; Things fall apart. (I am pretty sure I have used them all in a tight corner.)

In this category one thing guaranteed to upset some of you is the (mis)use of the phrase from the Gospel According to Saint Mark (King James Version): '10:13 And they brought young children to him, that he should touch them: and his disciples rebuked those that brought them. 10:14 But when Jesus saw it, he was much displeased, and said unto them, Suffer the little children to come unto me, and forbid them not: for of such is the kingdom of God.' A modern English version puts the relevant part like this: 'Let the little children come to me and do not try to stop them.'

A cliche is a cliche and perhaps it is one of its characteristics that it is detached from its original meaning. In Collins, the Guardian's preferred dictionary, to be consulted in the absence of any note in the style guide, as in this case, it is the fifth definition. Suffer: (archaic), to permit someone to do something, 'suffer the little children to come unto me'.

The following headline, which appeared this week, 'Suffer the little children – Sats revolt looms', prompted this slightly weary protest from a reader: 'Could someone please (please) tell Guardian writers to avoid the vulgar misuse of Mark 10:14 ... Can this injunction not be put on some message board or something – for all to see?'

There are two principal objections to it; one, that it is a disrespectful mucking about with a resonant phrase from the King James Version, and, two, that it simply appears much too often. Fairly recently we have had, 'Suffer little children – Leahy tells how Tesco got to be open all hours', and 'Suffer little children' on a report about rising costs of daycare for working parents. Sometimes the ironic intent is more apparent than others. The long-suffering reader would be happier if we abandoned it.

May 17 2003

The deeper recesses of the postbag

The following item appeared in our daily corrections column recently: 'We inserted an apostrophe into Goldsmiths College, in a letter [to the editor]. It does not have one. Sorry.' That may seem like a very small matter indeed, and hardly one to merit an apology. The correction was made in response to this email: 'Thank you for publishing my letter ... and for editing it so nicely. It was a pity, though, that you inserted an apostrophe in Goldsmiths. If you have a look at the one-foot-high stone lettering over the college entrance you will find there is no apostrophe in Goldsmiths College.

'As it happens, I suffer from mild dyslexia, and am militantly opposed to spelling fetischism [sic]. My friends like to tease me about this, particularly when it comes to apostrophes. Even now they will be chortling at my expense ... So when I saw you had inserted a spelling mistake, I was seriously indignified for at least 10 seconds. Please issue a correction.'

Coincidentally, I received a fax suggesting that this weekly column should appear occasionally under the byline of Mayes na gCopaleen, a reference to that incomparable humorist and humanist Myles na Gopaleen, also known as Myles na gCopaleen and Flann O'Brien (real name Brian O'Nolan). It will come as no surprise that he had some pertinent comments on the intrusive apostrophe (The Best of Myles by Flann O'Brien, published by Flamingo):

'In this month's "Bell" I am asked to accept as authoritative and penetrating an article on James Joyce. Throughout the piece the master's last work is consistently referred to as "Finnegan's Wake". That apostrophe (I happen to know) hastened Mr Joyce's end.'

There is no apostrophe, of course, in Finnegans Wake (the use of 'of course' was a particular annoyance to the Irish master).

The reference to Flann O'Brien came from a valued regular correspondent whose main point was this: 'That was a beauty of a mixed metaphor on yesterday's front page, "Berlusconi's regret at Nazi jibe defuses diplomatic stand-off." A stand-off doesn't appear to me to have the same threatening character as a bomb, grenade or other fuse- bearing weapon. In fact, is not a "stand-off" in itself a pause or drawing back in a conflict, so that it was the dispute itself which would have been "defused" by Berlusconi's apology?'

He finished with an O'Brien-ism: 'In what direction shall I shut? Up.'

Another correspondent this week began his email, 'At the risk of sounding like an old pedant … can you do anything about the use of the awful phrase "meet with" in the Guardian? Today it appears in the splash, "Mr Soames met with the MI6 director", and I despair. It's not the fact that it's an Americanism I object to, but the use of two words when one word – met – will do. What's more, there is already a proper use of "meet with" in English – meaning to experience or suffer – as in Kipling's "If you can meet with triumph and disaster."'

I mention these light matters because they make the job tenable. Occasionally things get out of hand.

Here's part of an email from a reader who had argued that an editorial sympathetic to a limited compromise on hunting rather than an outright ban explained why the paper had chosen to publish, the previous day, a picture of the pro-hunting rather than the anti-hunting demonstration outside the Commons. I wrote back to say that was nonsense. Now, read on:

'The sheer gall. There are two demos, one pro and one anti. Your paper reports only one of them, with a big picture of two girls with their tits out, while omitting to report the other demo altogether. The next day, it makes clear that editorially it's pro the cause of the demonstration it reported … you stupidly imply I'm making an argument based on retrogressive causation, which you call "nonsense".

'What does a lazy and smug traffic-warden type expect other than insults, when they tell someone they're arguing something they're not, so as to call it "complete nonsense"? I bet you thought your "if I may say so" was sophisticated, too.

'You must think it's one hell of a dignified position, to be the justifier and occasional in-house "criticism accepter" for your bosses. Do you practise in front of a mirror? Others might opine that it was a position that only a twerp would want, and only an arsehole wouldn't chuck in.'

I conclude with another quotation from Flann O'Brien: 'Let there be no more of this nonsense.'

July 19 2003

Tea, testicles and titters

One of the bonuses for readers of the Guardian's daily corrections column is that they often get, as a welcome interruption in the litany of more serious matters, something that makes them laugh aloud – always at the paper's expense, of course. Particularly hilarious and embarrassing confessions are seized upon and widely circulated.

In the past 10 days one of them has been broadcast to the nation by the Radio 4 Today programme and reprinted in the Times, and two have been picked up by the Londoner's Diary in the Evening Standard. (We are happy to provide this service but I do wonder – just a thought in passing – why the popularity of these gaffes with other newspapers does not encourage a systematic scouring of their own pages.)

Sometimes these things tremble between comedy and tragedy. What if the person we misquoted had actually said and meant the words attributed to him? From the following correction, which appeared this week, no one would think for a moment that the words had actually been uttered, even ironically:

'In our interview with Sir Jack Hayward, the chairman of Wolverhampton Wanderers, page 20, sport, yesterday, we mistakenly attributed to him the following comment: "Our team was the worst in the First Division and I'm sure it'll be the worst in the Premier League." Sir Jack had just declined the offer of a hot drink. What he actually said was: "Our tea was the worst in the First Division and I'm sure it'll be the worst in the Premier League." Profuse apologies.'

This was no mishearing by the journalist who interviewed Sir Jack. It was in the editing that, in a brief lapse of attention, someone saw 'tea' in an interview with the chairman of the newly promoted football team, and added the fateful 'm'.

Something similar may have happened to necessitate the

correction that followed this: 'A deletion in editing meant that we misquoted Sir Alex Ferguson on the transfer of Seba Veron, page 5, sport, August 9. What Sir Alex said was "Seba didn't not want to go" (did not not want to go). This appeared as "Seba did not want to go," something more positive and different in meaning.'

The other correction that enjoyed a circulation beyond the pages of the Guardian involved testicles. (In calling this up electronically I found there had been 200 references to testicles in the Guardian in the past couple of years. Here is one at random, on a perfectly serious matter: 'Hamsters and rats are brought into the surgery with suspected cancerous lumps, when what they actually have are testicles.')

The correction itself read: 'In an article about the adverse health effects of certain kinds of clothing, pages 8 and 9, G2, August 5, we omitted a decimal point when quoting a doctor on the optimum temperature of testicles. They should be 2.2 degrees Celsius below core body temperature, not 22 degrees lower.'

One reader had written: 'Even wearing your testicles outside your trousers would be unlikely to produce a reduction of 22 degrees centigrade from the core body temperature. Perhaps portable miniature air conditioning units would be the answer.'

This correction reminded me of one we did earlier (December 20 2000) in the same general area: 'A misprint of "public" in the Saturday Review resulted in Neville Cardus [the Guardian's late cricket correspondent and music critic] being quoted as writing on Shaw: "We had been repressed so long in our pubic discussions ... an hour of it and not a fumble."'

With errors of this kind cropping up not infrequently it is little wonder that the journalist's deliberate witticism is sometimes suspected by readers of being just another accident.

In a recent story about 'a dramatic increase in the sale of home bakery machines' to men, the paper's Northern editor wrote: 'Helped by roll models like the actor Terence Stamp, a keen baker, the British home bread market is now worth some £245m ...'

Half a dozen or so readers emailed. 'The item in today's paper about bread making machines referred to Terence Stamp as a "roll" model. Maybe the journalist responsible will claim it as a splendid pun, but I suspect it was more likely an unintended homophone. Please tell the offending person to use their loaf next time.'

I questioned the reporter about this. He insisted it was a gag and that he had left it like that after considering, and deciding against, enclosing the word roll in quotation marks. I believe him.

August 16 2003

Index

Index